THE HIDDEN 9/11 BLOOD TRAIL – WEATHER WARFARE AND THE BLOODY JACKPOT IN VEGAS

BY ROBERT J. ANTONELLIS

(BOOK I)

Copyright © 2024 by Robert J. Antonellis
Published by Spirit of America - Rising LLC

All rights reserved. No part of this publication may be reproduced, distributed, or transmitted in any form or by any means, including photocopying, recording, or other electronic or mechanical methods, without the prior written permission of the publisher.

For permission requests regarding photocopying, recording, storage, or retrieval systems, please direct all inquiries in writing to the author.

This publication represents the views and interpretations of the author and is intended to inform, engage, and provoke thought on the topics discussed.

DEDICATION

To those whose lives were cut short by an evil and invisible hand:

The victims of September 11, 2001—the thousands who perished in the towers, at the Pentagon, and on Flight 93; the first responders who gave everything to save others; and the families whose lives were forever changed.

To those who suffered in the wake of destruction carried by storms like Harvey, Irma, and Maria—victims of what we now recognize as Weather Warfare, and to those caught in the grip of orchestrated violence from Las Vegas to Benghazi, whose tragedies form the dark links of the *9/11 Blood Trail*.

To the innocents sacrificed by forces that profit from chaos and fear, whose truths are buried beneath layers of deceit and whose stories deserve the light of justice. From New York to New Orleans, from Shanksville to the Route 91 Harvest Festival, from the winds of destruction to the cries for accountability—we remember you.

This book is for those who refuse to accept simple lies and convenient narratives, who seek the connections between man-made disasters and hidden agendas, and who demand answers about the forces shaping our world from behind the shadows.

To those who understand that the battle for truth is a marathon, not a sprint, and who will not rest until the coldest of cold cases are reopened, investigated, and resolved with clarity and courage.

May the truth be unearthed, may justice prevail, and may we honor those lost—not just with our memories, but with our determination to expose the truth and rebuild what was taken from us.

ACKNOWLEDGMENTS

This book is the result of my unyielding pursuit of truth. I have always believed in thinking for myself and resisting the influence of television and popular narratives. My father, calling TV "The Idiot Box" and "The Boob Tube," taught me early to question everything I heard and saw. Just because a story is widely accepted doesn't make it true—in fact, the bigger the lie, the harder it falls when exposed.

My research spans years of uncovering contradictions, connecting dots, and challenging the narratives pushed by those in power. It has been a deeply personal journey of following current events, identifying patterns, and delving into hidden histories to reveal the threads woven through decades of deception. The Route 91 Harvest Fest Massacre, a gruesome reenactment of the chaos intended during *Helter Skelter* and the Tate-LaBianca murders, unfolded on an even bloodier scale, underscoring the manipulation behind such events.

While much of this work has been my own, I owe a debt of gratitude to family, friends, and associates who share my distrust of the theatrical displays of power and the "coincidences" that align to further hidden agendas. Their support has been invaluable.

The ongoing threats to national unity, safety, and even our leaders have only strengthened my resolve. This book, *The Hidden 9/11 Blood Trail*, is part of my effort to shine a light on the dark forces that undermine our country's strength. From the horrors of September 11, 2001, to Weather Warfare and manipulated chaos, America's unfinished business must be confronted.

By exposing these truths and calling for justice, we can dismantle the shadow government and its corrosive influence. Only through clarity and courage can we rebuild a one-tier system of justice and save our great nation.

ABOUT THE AUTHOR

Robert J. Antonellis is an author, engineer, and investigative researcher renowned for his ability to unravel complex and concealed truths. Combining technical expertise with a passion for understanding hidden connections, Robert focuses on exposing the forces behind America's most tragic events and their profound implications on the nation's unity.

Born into a family of Reagan Democrats, Robert grew up questioning the official narratives surrounding major historical events. His curiosity deepened while researching modern tragedies and historical patterns, from 9/11 to the sinister undertones of Weather Warfare and orchestrated mass violence. His engineering background has equipped him with a unique problem-solving perspective, enabling him to decode patterns hidden in plain sight and connect the dots across seemingly unrelated events.

In his latest work, *The Hidden 9/11 Blood Trail: From Weather Warfare to Bloody Jackpot in Vegas*, Robert examines how catastrophic events—from the September 11 attacks to Benghazi to the Route 91 Harvest Fest Massacre—are linked through a deliberate agenda to weaken the nation. He further explores the chilling role of Weather Warfare in advancing a broader scheme of fear and division.

The Hidden 9/11 Blood Trail is more than a book; it's a call to action for every American to uncover the truths that have been hidden for far too long. Robert invites readers to engage with his extensive research and join him in the fight for justice, unity, and a brighter future for the nation.

Stay tuned!

TABLE OF CONTENTS

SECTION 1 - THE AMERICAN CENTURY 7

THE URGENCY BEHIND THIS BOOK 8

WHY 9/11? 11

THE ANCIENT 9/11 BLOOD TRAIL 13

THE AMERICAN 9/11 BLOOD TRAIL 20

THE "AMERICAN CENTURY" 27

THE HIDDEN HAND 35

SECTION 2 - THE POST-AMERICAN CENTURY 47

GENOCIDE ART 48

BUSH 43 & THE GOATS 60

BENGHAZI – ANOTHER INSIDE JOB 70

WEATHER WARFARE ON THE U.S.A. 76

VIETNAM, WEATHER WARFARE & THE USSR 85

ROUTE "91" HARVEST FEST MASSACRE 89

SECTION 1
THE AMERICAN CENTURY

CHAPTER 1
THE URGENCY BEHIND THIS BOOK

On the afternoon of September 11, 2001, after being sent home from work, I found myself sitting on a hill in Arlington, Massachusetts, overlooking the Boston skyline. The air was eerily still, yet thick with a tension I'd never felt before. Like so many others that day, I braced for what seemed inevitable—another attack. In my mind, the threats were clear and immediate, something foreign and external, like the planes that had just devastated New York City and Washington, D.C.

I didn't know it then, but my understanding of the events unfolding around me was incomplete—simplistic, even. At the time, it was easy to believe the narrative being delivered: Osama bin Laden was the mastermind, terrorism was the weapon, and America had been caught off guard. But years of digging and researching would lead me to a far more disturbing realization. The truth was not just more complex; it was deliberately obscured.

The 9/11 attacks were not isolated acts of terrorism, nor were they the sole cause of the chaos that followed. They were the start—or perhaps the continuation—of a much larger pattern: a series of interconnected events designed not only to terrify but to destabilize. I call this pattern the *9/11 Blood Trail*. It is a thread that winds through some of America's darkest hours, from orchestrated disasters to calculated acts of violence, connecting seemingly unconnected tragedies into a single, sinister narrative.

On that hill in Arlington, I could never have imagined how deep this trail would go, or how far back its roots stretched. But as this book will reveal, the forces behind 9/11, Weather Warfare, and other events have worked tirelessly to erode national unity and reshape the very foundation of America. This is their hidden history—and exposing it is the first step toward reclaiming our own.

Why has the date 9/11 been systematically erased from public awareness? Who has done this, and what is their agenda? These questions go beyond the scope of this book, but in these pages, expect to be astonished by what you uncover. These events may seem almost unbelievable, especially when you realize the significant roles they have played.

For instance, on September 11, 1776, during the Staten Island "Peace" Conference, the British demanded that John Adams and Ben Franklin retract the Declaration of Independence, which had been signed by John Hancock just 69 days earlier. The answer was a resolute "No," and the war for freedom continued. But, the demand, on 9/11 appears to have been a "your money or your life" kind of threat. So, one year later, the same British General, Howe, attacked the capital, at that time.

Exactly one year later, on September 11, 1777, the British launched a fierce attack on George Washington at the Battle of Brandywine, forcing the Continental Army into a retreat northward to regroup and train for the winter in Yorktown Heights. Meanwhile, the British seized Philadelphia—the so-called "City of Brotherly Love."

During the Revolutionary War, there were a total of five separate 9/11 attacks by the British on Americans. Two of these attacks involved "Fake Indians"—white men dressed as Native Americans. This tactic was used by loyalists to the British Crown to conceal their true identities while expressing hatred for the Continental Army's vision of a Constitutional Republic that would replace the reign of King George III throughout the 13 colonies.

In the upcoming chapters, you'll uncover how each of these 9/11 events interconnects to form what I call the 9/11 Blood Trail—a complex and dark narrative that culminates in the Route 91 Harvest Festival Massacre, the final chapter of this book. This tragic event, which occurred on October 1, 2017, in Las Vegas, left 413 people wounded and 58 dead at the scene. Tragically, two more victims succumbed to their injuries later, bringing the total number of fatalities to 60.

The massacre unfolded within plain sight of the Luxor Hotel, the world's third-largest Egyptian pyramid, with its iconic Luxor Sky Beam piercing the night sky—a beam that some believe holds symbolic significance far beyond its architectural grandeur. Rooted in the mystique of ancient Egyptian and Islamic culture, the Luxor's towering presence and brilliant light have led some to view it as more than just a hotel, but as a modern-day symbol reflecting deeper historical and cultural themes.

Could it be just a coincidence that the massacre unfolded in the shadow of the Luxor's towering 140-foot Egyptian obelisk and its 110-foot-high replica of the Great Sphinx of Giza? What if there's a deeper story behind these symbolic structures and the events that occurred?

This book seeks to provide victims and all Americans with the vital evidence necessary to finally break the information deadlock that has long hindered the pursuit of justice in the deadliest mass shooting in modern U.S. history. By tracing the massacre's link to the 9/11 Blood Trail, I will expose how this event is interconnected with other major developments, all part of a broader chain of events: the New World Order Speech on September 11, 1990, the devastating attacks of September 11, 2001, the clandestine use of Weather Warfare, and even the attack on the U.S. Consulate in Benghazi on September 11, 2012. Each of these incidents is tied to a deeper, hidden agenda that has shaped global politics and the pursuit of power for decades.

The truth behind these tragedies has been hidden—until now. Understanding these events is essential if we are to move forward as a unified and safe nation. As a reader, you have the right to know what truly happened—and, more importantly, why.

CHAPTER 2
WHY 9/11?

Many people still believe the narrative that "Osama bin Laden and al-Qaeda selected September 11 as the date for the attacks as a symbolic statement, intending to create a parallel between the emergency phone number '911' and the chaos and panic the attacks would cause."

This assertion falsely presumes that bin Laden had the autonomy to make such a decision about the timing of the attacks and that the "911" sequence was randomly chosen by AT&T as the emergency number. However, this simplification ignores a much larger, more sinister reality. The 9/11 attacks on the World Trade Center Towers and the Pentagon had direct involvement from elements within the U.S. Government, with bin Laden playing a minor, almost insignificant role. By the time the 911 emergency system went live in 1968, the numbers "911" were already deeply rooted in symbolism, dating back thousands of years, as you will soon discover.

In other words, the American public has been deceived on multiple fronts. This systematic manipulation has been orchestrated by politicians, the "Mainstream Media," and other entities, all working to undermine our ability to recognize and respond to direct threats against the United States of America. One prominent example of this deception can be seen in the Route 91 Harvest Festival Massacre, which, along with other 9/11-attacks, hiding in plain sight.

As you delve deeper into the 9/11 Blood Trail, you will see how established 9/11 events connect directly to the Route 91 Harvest Fest Massacre, revealing that it was orchestrated by Domestic Islamic Terrorists embedded within our own government, and beyond.

Modern Freemasonry has existed for over 300 years, but its symbolic and philosophical foundations extend much further back, drawing on the traditions of medieval stonemasons' guilds and possibly even older teachings.

To understand the significance of the numbers "911," one must first consider their meaning within the Occult and secret societies like the Freemasons. Twin columns, for example, are regarded as a "symbol of strength and stability" in Masonic teachings. As master builders for thousands of years, Freemasons have constructed their organizations around symbolic tools and artifacts such as the Compass, the Square, the Masonic Apron, and the Gavel—even the Letter "G" holds profound meaning in their rituals.

In Freemasonry, the number 9 signifies fulfillment, completion, and spiritual enlightenment. When combined with 11, it takes on a darker interpretation. The number 911 can be seen as representing "an extreme challenge to strength and stability," suggesting turmoil, chaos, or a disruption of order.

This framework allows us to explore a deeper theory: Could the infamous number 911, which became America's universal emergency code, have been deliberately chosen with these symbolic meanings in mind? Were the Freemasons, with their deep-rooted symbolism, already entrenched in the U.S. Government at that time? Or sooner? And if so, are they among those who suppress information about possible government involvement in the 9/11 attacks?

If 911 means "extreme" challenge to strength and stability, might "91" simply mean "challenge to strength and stability?" What about the Route 91 Harvest Festival Massacre?

CHAPTER 3
THE ANCIENT 9/11 BLOOD TRAIL

The 9/11 Blood Trail represents a chilling and recurring pattern of surprise attacks and brutal acts of violence that have left a bloody imprint across the globe throughout recorded history. This trail traces its origins back to the ancient world, weaves through centuries of conflict, and even connects America's founding to some of the world's earliest and most catastrophic struggles. The 9/11 Blood Trail exposes a deep-seated animosity against Western Civilization that has long simmered within certain Islamic societies and pro-Islamic factions, as well as among powerful secret societies scattered across the world. These societies have injected anti-Semitic and anti-Christian hatred into the very fabric of Western society, distorting its values and principles, and creating False Flag operations, creating mayhem and death, while hiding their own involvement.

Entities like the Freemasons, Rosicrucians, Skull and Bones, and the Knights of Eulogia revere and wield these symbolic numbers—911—using them in rituals and operations to exert influence. Members of these societies often ascend to the highest echelons of power globally, wielding control over people as effectively as the Kings and Queens of old. But why do these numbers continue to appear in such dark and destructive contexts? Could they signify more than just a date? Are they markers of a deeper agenda, one that shapes history from the shadows?

The Ancient Origins of 9/11 Symbolism

Take a closer look at <u>Table 3.1</u> and note the two gold squares in the upper left corner, highlighting the destruction of the First and

13

Second Temples of Jerusalem. Both temples were completely destroyed by fire on the 9th day of Av, the 11th month on the Hebrew calendar. This tragic and symbolic date, which translates to 9/11, has been etched into the Jewish faith for over 2,600 years.

In 586 BC, King Nebuchadnezzar of Babylon ordered the destruction of the First Temple of Jerusalem on the 9th day of Av, marking the earliest documented 9/11 massacre in our history. This event established a recurring pattern, connecting the passion for persecuting the Jewish people on 9/11 to the occult practices of ancient Babylon. However, this pattern didn't end with the Babylonians. The Romans, who later destroyed the Second Temple, also had their own occult practices and numerology, using the same digits to express their dominion and hatred.

In 70 AD, Emperor Titus Vespasian commanded the destruction of the Second Temple of Jerusalem on the 9th day of Av, 11th month, cementing a cycle of bloodshed and destruction that has left an indelible mark on the Jewish faith. To this day, Tisha B'Av (the "ninth of Av") is an annual day of fast in Judaism, commemorating the destruction of both temples and symbolizing a time of profound mourning and reflection. Could these ancient events, locked into this recurring 9/11 date, hold the key to understanding modern atrocities?

The Modern Echoes of Ancient Hatred

This ancient pattern of destruction, used by both the Babylonians and the Romans, still resonates in today's world events. It has been revived and echoed in recent tragedies, such as the Route 91 Harvest Festival Massacre, a devastating attack that targeted a predominantly Christian audience. Incredibly, even this modern atrocity shares a connection to the enduring 9/11 symbolism. Why is it that these numbers continue to surface in the context of human tragedy? And how deeply are these patterns ingrained in the power structures that influence world events today?

As you explore the chapters in this book, you'll uncover the dark undercurrents of the 9/11 Blood Trail and how these symbolic numbers have been weaponized by those who seek to spread chaos and destruction. Could this recurring date be more than just a coincidence? Could it be part of a deliberate design—a signal used by those who operate in the shadows, hidden in plain sight?

What do these symbols truly mean? Who benefits from repeating this pattern of bloodshed and despair? And how does this ancient animosity still impact us today? Keep these questions in mind as you delve deeper into the next chapters. The answers may challenge everything you thought you knew about history, power, and the forces that shape our world.

911 Blood Trail Pattern

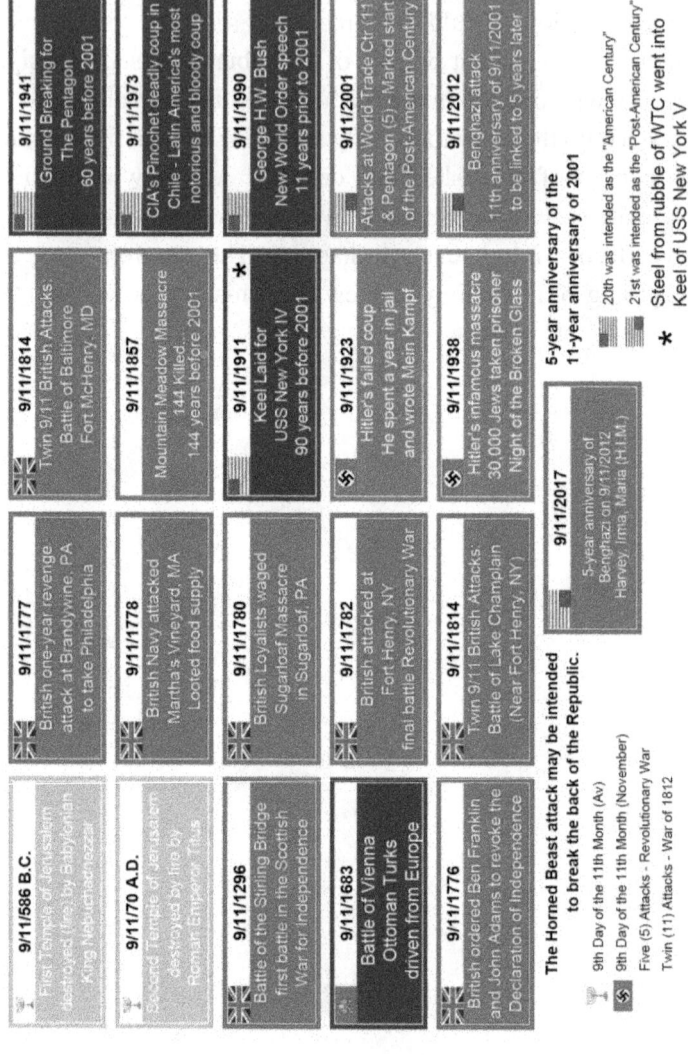

Table 3.1 - 911 Blood Trail Pattern

A Closer Look at Historical Patterns

There are numerous historical examples that demonstrate the importance of the numeric sequence "9/11" to those who seek to inflict destruction. The date itself is secondary to the symbolic power of these numbers. Consider Adolf Hitler, a known occultist, who formed the Nazi Party with the help of members from the Masonic Thule Society, an organization that promoted a mix of Teutonic mythology, racial purity, and anti-Semitic ideas. Hitler orchestrated two of his most significant attacks on the 9th day of the 11th month, using Germany's date format—day, month, year—where November 9th is written as 9/11. This further illustrates that the true significance lies in the demonic mythology and numerology of "9/11" rather than in specific calendar dates, with anti-Semitism playing a critical role, as it aligns with key dates on the Hebrew calendar. Occultists like Hitler ascribe powerful meanings to these numbers, symbolizing an "extreme challenge to strength and stability."

On November 9, 1923 (9/11/23), Hitler initiated his infamous Beer Hall Putsch, a failed coup attempt against the Weimar Republic. This event resulted in 20 deaths before Hitler's arrest, after which he calmly stayed in a bar, drinking beer, awaiting the authorities. During his imprisonment, he wrote his manifesto, Mein Kampf. Although this coup wasn't a direct assault on Germany's Jewish community, it was still a 9/11 attack using the German date format and took place on the same day as Tisha B'Av—a significant day of mourning in Judaism.

On November 9, 1938 (9/11/38), Hitler launched his single most devastating day of attacks on Germany's Jewish population—Kristallnacht, or the "Night of Broken Glass." Over 30,000 Jews were violently dragged from their homes and sent to concentration camps, where many were immediately executed in gas chambers. Nearly 2,000 synagogues were set ablaze—some as grand and historically significant as New York's St. Patrick's Cathedral.

Witnesses were horrified as fire departments were deployed—not to extinguish the flames consuming the synagogues—but to ensure that the fire didn't spread to adjacent buildings. This 20th-century manifestation of hatred can be traced back to the mystical date of 9/11, linking Hitler's atrocities to the ancient patterns of destruction practiced by the Babylonians and Romans.

The Broader Historical Context

This obsession with the 9/11 sequence isn't limited to Nazi numerology; it predates even National Socialism. Consider the Battle of Stirling Bridge on 9/11/1296, during Scotland's First War of Independence. Or take the Battle of Vienna on 9/11/1683, where the combined forces of King Jan III Sobieski of Poland and Pope Innocent XI defeated the Ottoman Turks, saving Europe from a potential Islamic conquest.

In Table 3.1 (which I created in 2017), the bottom square—dated 9/11/2017—illustrates an anticipated 9/11 attack. This figure specifies the "When, Who, and Why" but leaves the "What and How" vague, awaiting the actual event to unfold. I made this chart in 2017 after predicting that a 9/11-style attack would occur that year, as you will read more about in the upcoming chapters.

Later in this book, you'll discover what that attack was and how it connects to the unprecedented dumping of 40 trillion gallons of water by Hurricane Helene. Far from being a natural disaster or the result of Global Warming, it wasn't an Act of God either. Instead, it was something far more sinister—an event intricately connected to the same ancient patterns of destruction and hatred that have echoed throughout history. This book reveals an irrefutable connection between Weather Warfare and the 9/11 Blood Trail, exposing depths of depravity that go far beyond the actions of the Deep State, ultimately tracing back to Satanic secret societies that have long exerted influence over world affairs.

So, in order to fully grasp the brutal intentions behind the 9/11 Blood Trail that weaves its way through America today, one must first understand that it is not a new phenomenon. It is, in fact, a continuation of the certifiably anti-Semitic 9/11 Blood Trail that originated in the ancient world and has persisted through the ages—reaching a tragic climax in the modern era. As covered in this chapter, the hatred and symbolism embedded in these events reflect a deep-rooted enmity towards Christianity and Western Civilization that has been nurtured and wielded by shadowy forces long before American was founded.

CHAPTER 4

THE AMERICAN 9/11 BLOOD TRAIL

The American people have unwittingly been misled about the history of 9/11 attacks on America. This deception is perpetuated through the "misinformation and disinformation" disseminated by a Fake "Mainstream Media," politicians who hide and obscure the truth, and history professors more concerned with securing tenure than doing their duty—enlightening and educating the student body.

Basel "Ayman" Hamdan, a producer at MSNBC, revealed a grim truth to the O'Keefe Media Group in hidden camera footage: "They [MSNBC] have made their viewers dumber over the years." Yet, no matter which channel you choose to watch, or what podcast you listen to, a veil of ignorance continues to obscure the Hidden 9/11 Blood Trail—a sinister thread that winds through global history, seeping into America's past, and leaving behind a path marred by death and destruction. This ignorance isn't confined to any one channel; it's a widespread blindness that distorts the narrative of these pivotal events.

You've already read about the British Crown's relentless pursuit of attacking Americans throughout the Revolutionary War, particularly on the fateful date of September 11th. Refer to Table 4.1, where each attack in the first column (the 18th Century) is marked by a British Union Jack flag in the upper left corner, including the first two attacks in the 19th Century. Although the last two 9/11 attacks of the Revolutionary War did not involve British Red Coats, they were carried out by Native American "Indians" and "Fake Indians" who betrayed their fellow Americans.

One such tragedy was the Sugarloaf Massacre, which took place along Little Nescopeck Creek on 9/11/1780. This battle saw Iroquois Indians and Tory Loyalists—people who identified as American—murdering and cannibalizing American militiamen. This was the bloodiest battle of the Revolutionary War, and it took place at the hands of those who betrayed the principles of American independence.

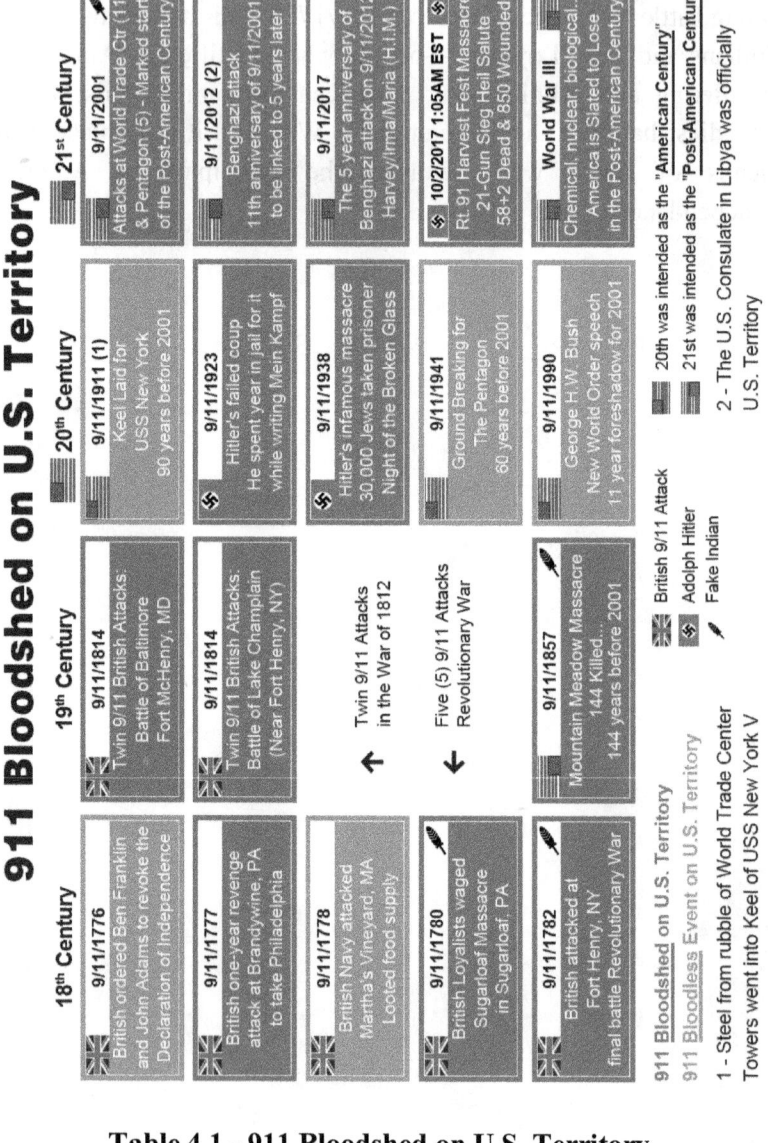

Table 4.1 - 911 Bloodshed on U.S. Territory

Occult Connections and Curious Proximities

Jay Parker, of Matrix Warriors, has exposed a "strong concentration of occult activity and Dupont loyalists from Southeastern Pennsylvania down to Northern Delaware." Yet, my research places this occult corridor even further north, extending up to Scranton, PA—the birthplace of Joseph Robinette Biden.

This link is partly due to the eerie proximity of the Sugarloaf Massacre, which occurred just 33 miles south-southwest of Scranton, Pennsylvania. Could this closeness be purely coincidental? Or does it hint at something more sinister lurking beneath the surface?

◆ **Did you know? Pennsylvania is called the Keystone State and has been since its founding. In architecture, a keystone is the central stone at the top of an arch and is the final piece placed during construction because it locks all the other stones into position. Symbolically, in Freemasonry, the keystone represents completion and perfection.**

The "Fake Indians" from the Revolutionary War could arguably be considered the forerunners of today's Democratic Party. This may explain why not a single Democrat criticizes Elizabeth Warren for her false claims of "Cherokee heritage." Notice the 19th Century, and the 9/11/1857 massacre of 144 Americans, known as the Mountain Meadows Massacre. This was the last 9/11 attack on U.S. territory until the catastrophic 9/11 attacks of 2001—exactly 144 years later.

It's as if that same hatred for America leaped over the 20th Century, which was supposed to be "The American Century," only to resurface violently at the dawn of the 21st Century—a period now marked as "The Post-American Century." What a tragic and ominous start to a new millennium!

◆ **Did you ever learn any of this in school?**

Notice, all of the American based events in the 20th Century had an upright American flag in the upper left corner, while every box in the 21st Century has an inverted American flag. You will come to read why the 20th Century was preordained as the "American Century," in this chapter.

Twin British 9/11 Attacks to Divide and Conquer

The War of 1812 is one of the most misunderstood conflicts in American history. It's been presented by historians—and likely your history teachers—in such a dull and uninspired way that it makes students' eyes glaze over. But when you follow the 9/11 Blood Trail, a very different picture emerges—one that will keep you wide awake and alert.

King George III reigned in England for nearly 60 years, from 1760 to 1820, making him one of the longest-reigning British monarchs in history. He was King during the buildup to the War for Independence, throughout the Revolutionary War itself, and throughout the entirety of the War of 1812.

The colonists hated King George III for many reasons, including the oppressive Stamp Act, which levied unbearable taxes on essential goods. They despised the concept of "Taxation without Representation" and abhorred the Coercive Acts—measures designed to punish Massachusetts for the Boston Tea Party and reassert British authority over the colonies.

After America declared independence, King George III's private letters and personal papers reveal a complex mix of regret, frustration, and a lingering hope for reconciliation. He expressed deep disappointment over the loss of what he referred to as "the brightest jewel in his crown."

◆ **Do you really believe that one of the richest and most powerful men on earth would simply let go of his beloved 13 colonies, without a fight? After all, he was known to call the colonies his "American Plantation."**

Let's follow the 9/11 Blood Trail and see how the War of 1812—the second war in which British Red Coats fought on American soil—allows us to classify 9/11 attacks on America as "Royal Revenge."

Could these two wars be interconnected, at least in the eyes of the British? And if so, what do these connections reveal about the forces at play behind America's most catastrophic attacks?

Star-Spangled Banner

Before diving into the two pivotal 9/11 attacks during the War of 1812, let's first revisit the origins of the Star-Spangled Banner.

You probably know that Francis Scott Key penned the Star-Spangled Banner—America's National Anthem—on the morning after a relentless British naval assault. He wrote it upon seeing the giant American flag still flying proudly over Fort McHenry. You may also know that the British bombardment was concentrated on this fort, which successfully prevented the formidable British warships from breaching Baltimore Harbor. But what you might not know is that this critical battle began on a date that holds special significance: September 11, 1814.

History reveals that the residents of Baltimore seemed to grasp something that many of today's historians overlook—the war was not just a skirmish over territory. King George III launched this campaign with one goal in mind: to re-subjugate America and completely undo the results of the Revolutionary War—our hard-fought War for Independence.

What a terrifying prospect—an overt Counter-Revolution to reclaim America, the prized jewel of King George III's empire.

Connecting the Dots: The 9/11 Blood Trail

So, what ties these two wars together? There are several connections, but two stand out: the names of the forts and, more importantly, the dates themselves.

Interestingly, the fort names—Fort Henry during the Revolutionary War and Fort McHenry during the War of 1812—share a resemblance. But a more striking link is found in the dates, which are directly connected by the 9/11 Blood Trail: September 11, 1782, and September 11, 1814.

But the connections don't end there. In <u>Table 4.1</u>, notice a second 9/11 attack during the War of 1812: a British naval strike on Lake Champlain, just 88 miles (as the crow flies) from Fort Henry. This battle, known as the Battle of Plattsburgh, took place concurrently with the Battle of Baltimore.

A victory for the British in either of these battles—the Battle of Baltimore or the Battle of Plattsburgh—would have split the young United States in two, tipping the scales of the war and potentially drawing the country back into the grasp of the British Crown.

From Defeat to Unity: A Nation's Anthem

These twin defeats inflicted on the formidable British Navy sparked a surge of patriotism across America. The nation found itself singing a new anthem—The Star-Spangled Banner—a song that captured the indomitable spirit of the American people as they united in the face of adversity.

Put simply, the War of 1812 was not just another war; it was a calculated British Royal Counter-Revolution aimed at overturning the freedoms we won during the American Revolution. As you'll discover, the 9/11 Blood Trail continues to weave its way through American history, with the same age-old hatred seeking to purge Christianity, Judaism, and Patriotism from our continent—threats that remain very real to this day.

◆ **Did you know? The British still celebrate the day the British Red Coats burned the White House?**

CHAPTER 5
THE "AMERICAN CENTURY"

The 9/11 Blood Trail reveals that the War of 1812 was not an "Outcropping of the Napoleonic Wars, or simply a minor conflict over maritime rights or territorial expansion—it was, in fact, a full-fledged British Royal Counter-Revolution. King George III sought to reclaim the American colonies he had lost during the Revolutionary War, 32 years earlier. The War of 1812 was a desperate attempt to reassert British control over the continent.

The American Century: Was It Prefabricated?

Let's follow the 9/11 Blood Trail further to prove that the 20th Century was preordained to be the "American Century." Remarkably, there was no loss of life on American soil on September 11th from 1900 to 1999. It appears that the same forces which manufactured this period of peace in American history also laid the groundwork for the 21st Century to become the "Post-American Century," marked by tragedy and loss, beginning notably with the 9/11 attacks in 2001.

Throughout the 19th and 21st centuries, significant loss of life occurred on 9/11 due to British and other foreign attacks. But, strangely, the 20th Century stands apart as the only century in which 9/11 events did not involve direct attacks or fatalities on American soil. Instead, this period featured pivotal 9/11 events that indirectly shaped America's future.

Key 9/11 Events in the 20th Century

September 11, 1911 – The Rise of American Naval Power.
On this day, at the New York Navy Yard, the U.S. Navy laid down the keel of the USS New York (BB-34), the lead ship in her class.

This battleship represented a major leap forward in military technology, being the first U.S. Navy ship equipped with the powerful 14-inch/45-caliber guns. The USS New York would go on to play a key role in World War I, sinking a German U-boat in 1918—making it the only U.S. ship to do so during the war.

This 9/11 event was symbolic, boosting the United States' military capability at a critical time, just three years before the start of WWI. It foreshadowed the attacks on New York City, New York State, and the United States 90 years later, on 9/11/2001. The steel from the destroyed World Trade Center Towers was even used to build the fifth iteration of the USS New York, as if to acknowledge that "we've always been in charge."

◆ **Was this a subtle acknowledgment that those in power orchestrated it all—a quiet message that "we got away with it"?**

November 9, 1923 – Hitler's Coup Attempt
Known as the Beer Hall Putsch, Adolf Hitler's failed coup attempt against the Weimar Republic resulted in 20 deaths before his arrest. He spent the following year in jail, where he wrote his manifesto, Mein Kampf. Although this 9/11 event did not occur on American soil, it set in motion a series of events that would plunge the world into World War II.

November 9, 1938 – Kristallnacht
Hitler's single most devastating attack on Germany's Jewish population occurred on this date, also known as the Night of Broken Glass. Over 30,000 Jews were arrested and sent to concentration camps, while nearly 2,000 synagogues were destroyed, with some as grand as St. Patrick's Cathedral in New York City. Like the date of his coup, Hitler ordered Kristallnacht for a Jewish day of mourning called Tisha B'Av (the "ninth of Av").

September 11, 1941 – The Pentagon Groundbreaking

On this date, under President Franklin Delano Roosevelt's administration, construction began on the Pentagon—the future headquarters of the U.S. Department of Defense. The building would later become the site of one of the airliner attacks on 9/11/2001, exactly 60 years later.

◆ **Could those secretly working to build up the U.S. military have been the same ones who, decades later, orchestrated attacks to steal America's rocket, nuclear, and space technologies?**

The Hidden Symbolism of the Numbers 11, 5, and 69

I cracked the code of the New World Order, which the Hidden 9/11 Blood Trail reveals, is nothing less that the Ancient Order for the New World. So, contrary to popular belief, the NWO is far from New. It's us who are new, and where we live is the "New World." And for Conservatives and Patriots, they will agree, we are not behaving in a way that is "Orderly."

Let's start with the logic of the ancients, the Babylonians and the Romans...The number 11 recurs throughout the 9/11 Blood Trail. Today, 11 represents a Freemasonic symbol of "Strength and Stability," because it represent Twin Columns, which is a required element in constructing a doorway. But when combined in the sequence 911, the meaning transforms to represent "Extreme Challenge to Strength and Stability." These numbers have sinister connotations in occult and Masonic symbolism, extending back to ancient civilizations.

The Twin Towers, symbolizing "11," were attacked on the 11th day of September.

11 is also seen as a Satanic salute, represented by two fingers raised—a sign of defiance and Satanic power. See Image 4.1.

The 9/11 Blood Trail continues to unfold throughout history, revealing a dark and hidden agenda behind these significant events.

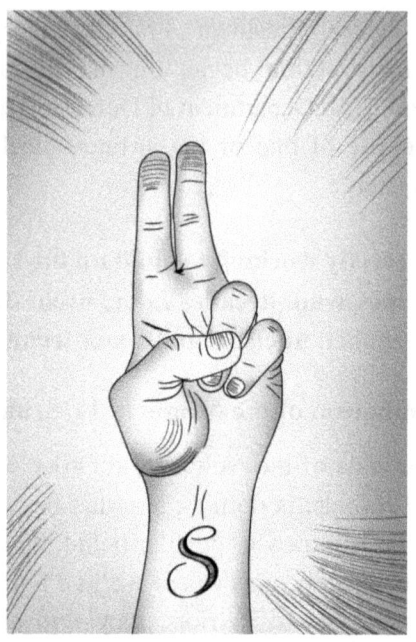

Image 4.1 The Sign of Satan

The Symbolism of "5" and D.C.'s Hidden Pentagram

The number 5 holds a significant place in this narrative. It is represented by the five corners of the Pentagon, the world's largest military headquarters, and is deeply ingrained in the symbolism of power and control. Does it signify Satanism?

But what else does it mean?

◆ **Is it shocking to see a Satanic symbol so close to the people's White House?**

Take a look at Image 4.2, which highlights a disturbing connection that many would prefer to ignore. This image reveals a hidden pentagram in the very layout of Washington, D.C., centered around the address of the White House, 1600 Pennsylvania Avenue. Notice the two key points marked on the map: Dupont Circle and

Logan Circle. Both these locations have connections to occult symbolism and secret societies.

Why might this dark plot exist so close to the center of American power? Could it be linked to the claims by Jay Parker, who speaks of an evil power source involving Pennsylvania, the Dupont family, and the occult? Let's take a deeper look.

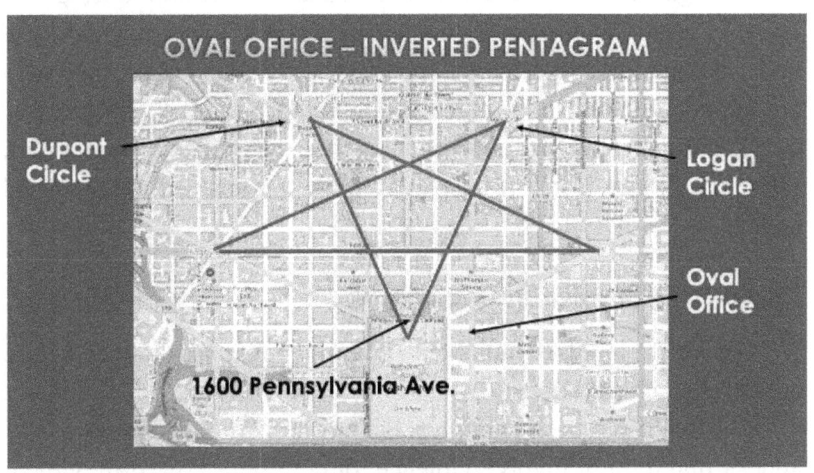

Image 4.2: The Hidden Pentagram in Washington, D.C.

Recall the controversial allegations surrounding the Logan Act—a never-before-used law that prohibits unauthorized U.S. citizens from negotiating with foreign governments. The first person to accuse Republicans of violating this obscure act was none other than then-Vice President Joe Biden. This accusation surfaced during the Democrat-led "Russia, Russia, Russia" campaign, which aimed to undermine President-elect Donald J. Trump's incoming administration in January 2017.

But what is the connection here? Where is the deeper meaning?

Who is Joe Biden, and where does he come from? He hails from Pennsylvania—just like the famous Pennsylvania Avenue. And which family is believed to have provided Biden with financial backing and influence? The Dupont Family, a name synonymous with power, wealth, and a history of involvement in American politics.

◆ **Could the Logan Act be a code for something darker, perhaps treason?**

Is Logan Circle named after this act, as if to celebrate it? Could this be a symbolic gesture from those who placed the pentagram right under the nose of the American people? And if this is true, then who are the people in power who celebrate Satanism at the very heart of our Republic? This "Fallen Angel" symbolism suggests that a dark influence is not just lurking—it's firmly entrenched in the Oval Office.

Deciphering the Significance of "69"

We've explored the numbers 11 and 5, but what about 69? Here are two key observations:

The sequence of events reveals that the 20th Century saw 9/11 attacks that did not involve violence, only to be followed by violent 9/11 attacks in the 21st Century. Specifically, there were 90-year forecasts (nine decades) and 60-year forecasts (six decades). The combination—6 and 9—represents another symbolic fingerprint left in plain sight.

Consider the British "demand to surrender" on 9/11/1776. This occurred exactly 69 days after July 4, 1776, Independence Day. Was John Hancock, the first signatory of the Declaration of Independence, subtly instructed to sign on that date? The timing suggests that even the founding of America was influenced by these occult forces—forces more powerful and insidious than the people ever realized.

Manufacturing the "American Century"

While no lives were lost on American soil on 9/11 during the entire 20th Century, there were still 9/11 events that shaped American dominance. The 20th Century was meticulously crafted to become the American Century—a period of prosperity and military strength.

Key 9/11 Events of the 20th Century

September 11, 1911: The keel of the USS New York was laid down at the New York Navy Yard. This significant advancement in naval technology foreshadowed the role of New York in later 9/11 attacks. Steel from the destroyed World Trade Center towers was even used to build the fifth iteration of the USS New York.

◆ **Was this a quiet nod from those in power, a whisper that "we're in charge—we've always been in charge"?**

November 9, 1923: Adolf Hitler's failed coup attempt, known as the Beer Hall Putsch, took place in Germany on 9/11 (November 9th, in German format). This was the beginning of a series of tragic 9/11 events that would later include Kristallnacht in 1938.

September 11, 1941: Groundbreaking for the Pentagon under President Franklin Delano Roosevelt. Sixty years later, the Pentagon was attacked by air on 9/11/2001. This coincidence was no accident—it was part of the preordained plan.

The 9/11 Attack in the 20th Century: Chile

September 11, 1973: The CIA and the Nixon Administration backed the deadliest coup in Latin America's history, where General Augusto Pinochet overthrew the democratically elected government of President Salvador Allende in Chile. The coup led to the establishment of a military dictatorship that lasted for nearly two decades, marked by widespread human rights abuses and bloodshed.

This event is marked in Table 3.1 with the American flag, signifying U.S. involvement. While it did not result in American casualties, it exemplifies the U.S.'s strategic maneuvering to maintain control and influence, keeping Americans safe while pursuing larger geopolitical objectives.

The 20th Century was preordained to be the American Century, allowing the U.S. to wage wars, build the greatest military in the world, and accumulate unparalleled global influence.

Wait until you see who benefited…

CHAPTER 6
THE HIDDEN HAND

In this chapter, we will explore the unsettling extent to which secret societies have infiltrated the highest levels of the United States federal government, the immense power they wield, and the depths of depravity they often reach, weakening America in the process. This chapter, along with those that follow, will trace a critical part of the Hidden 9/11 Blood Trail across three presidencies: beginning with George H.W. Bush (41), moving to his son George W. Bush (43), and culminating in the Obama/Biden/Clinton administration. We will also delve into the 9/11 Blood Trail's connection to weather manipulation and its role in the increasing weaponization of weather against the American people.

While seniors at Yale University, three generations of the Bush family—Prescott Bush in 1917, George H.W. Bush in 1948, and George W. Bush in 1968—were inducted into Skull and Bones, the secret society most deeply connected to the Deep State, the New World Order, and global elite networks. Skull and Bones is one of the most influential invitation-only secret societies, a breeding ground for presidents and powerful figures in commerce, communications, diplomacy, espionage, law, and politics. With over 2,500 members, primarily from wealthy northeastern families, it has shaped world affairs, with families like Bush, Ford, Goodyear, Harriman, Heinz, Kellogg, Phelps, Rockefeller, Taft, Vanderbilt, and Whitney having deep connections to its ranks.

The society's headquarters, known as The Tomb, is a windowless, fortress-like building at Yale, symbolizing its members' obsession with death. Rumors abound, including tales of a basement called the Morgue, allegedly filled with empty caskets used in initiation rituals.

New initiates, known as "Bonesmen," are said to confront death symbolically, internalizing the grave consequences of betraying the society's secrets.

◆ **Were Bush 41 and Bush 43 truly serving the American people during their presidencies, or were they concealing secrets and answering to Skull and Bones?**

There is a documented connection between Skull and Bones and the opium trade, which ties back to its roots at Yale University. Just 17 years after the end of the War of 1812, Skull and Bones was founded in 1832. The society's ties to the China opium trade trace back to its founders, including Samuel Russell, who had direct involvement through his relative William Huntington Russell, a key figure in the trade between India, Turkey, and China.

Today, the United States consumes over 80% of the world's opiates, but during the Opium Wars, American involvement in the global opium trade was focused on moving opium into China, devastating Chinese society while sparing the U.S. from widespread consumption. However, Boston played a significant role as a transshipment point for American merchants, like those from Russell & Company, who transported Chinese goods—such as tea, silk, and porcelain—obtained through opium trade routes. Many of these merchants, often connected to elite groups like Skull and Bones, maintained the facade of being "clean businessmen," despite the opium trade being the foundation of their immense fortunes. This trade wreaked havoc on China's population, leading to widespread addiction and societal collapse.

◆ **What was it about opium that captured the interest of the British Crown and their "offspring," Skull and Bones?**

Skull & Bones and China's "Century of Humiliation"

Many people know that Skull and Bones was founded by individuals from powerful American families involved in the Chinese opium trade. Notable families, like the Russell, Forbes, and Perkins families, had deep business interests in China. William Huntington Russell, co-founder of Skull and Bones in 1832, came from a family deeply involved in global shipping and international trade, including the opium trade with China.

These American families, particularly those associated with Russell & Company, worked alongside British merchants, including those from the British East India Company, to establish a triangular opium trade. This trade exploited China's growing addiction to opium while draining the country of its wealth. Although these merchants portrayed themselves as respectable businessmen, they profited from an industry that devastated China, fueling addiction and social collapse.

This triangular trade involved three primary legs:

First, American and British merchants used strong currencies, like the British pound and U.S. dollar, to purchase large quantities of opium from British-controlled India, which was then shipped to China.

Second, opium was exchanged in China for valuable goods, such as silver, silk, porcelain, tea, and spices, which were then shipped to Western markets, including Boston and other major American ports.

Finally, these luxury goods were sold in the West for significant profits, enriching the merchants involved.

This system was fueled by the growing opium addiction in China, which led to its "Century of Humiliation"—a period of societal collapse, foreign domination, and internal strife.

◆ **Was the social collapse of China part of the plan for the British and American groups behind the Chinese opium trade?**

Many of these American merchants, who purchased Chinese goods and works of art in exchange for opium, effectively enslaved Chinese workers and artists to their addiction. Opium is highly addictive, and once addicted, people experience intense cravings and debilitating withdrawal symptoms. This made many Chinese more likely to accept opium as payment for their labor, perpetuating the cycle of exploitation and addiction.

The legacy of the opium trade contributed significantly to weakening Chinese society, making it vulnerable to internal revolutions and foreign intervention. While the opium trade was not the sole factor, it created conditions that allowed movements like Mao Zedong's Communist Party to rise to power in 1949. Mao aggressively clamped down on the opium trade and rehabilitated addicts, ensuring the end of the China opium trade.

Today, China has relatively low opioid addiction compared to other countries, like the United States, where the opioid crisis has become a major public health issue. In an ironic twist, America now faces an addiction crisis fueled by fentanyl and the legalization of marijuana, which some believe is contributing to an American social collapse—one that could mirror China's earlier Century of Humiliation.

◆ **Is this the plan of the New World Order? To weaken America through addiction and create a society so destabilized that it might embrace global communism?**

So, doesn't it seem as though America and China have switched places regarding the future workforce of each nation? America's workers are increasingly falling under the weight of fentanyl addiction and the legalization of marijuana, with the accompanying risk of social collapse, perhaps reminiscent of China's Century of Humiliation. The shame of such an era in China was so profound that many people eventually embraced the Communist Revolution led by Mao Zedong.

◆ Could this be the plan of the New World Order—to use addiction as a tool to weaken American society, and, in its weakened state, present global communism as the only solution?

Prescott Bush and the Adolf Hitler Project

Prescott Bush, the grandfather of George W. Bush, had financial ties to Nazi Germany during World War II. Two of his businesses were shut down for violating the Trading with the Enemy Act, yet he continued to facilitate financial transactions through the Union Banking Corporation (UBC) and Swiss banks. These dealings helped fund the Nazi war machine and its unspeakable acts of genocide. This raises troubling questions about how deeply Fascist connections ran within the Bush family.

As previously mentioned, Hitler timed significant events, such as his failed coup attempt and Kristallnacht (Night of the Broken Glass), to align with the 9/11 Blood Trail: November 9, 1923, and November 9, 1938. These dates were likely chosen to symbolize a connection to the ominous 9/11 pattern and to secure continued financial backing from powerful interests, particularly in the United States. The Bush family's involvement in these patterns is further evidenced.

On September 11, 1990, President George H.W. Bush delivered his infamous New World Order speech to a Joint Session of Congress, in which he described a "new era, freer from the threat of terror." This speech marked a pivotal moment—the close of America's Century and the laying of groundwork for what would become the Post-American Century.

Bush 41 and 9/11 Satanic Numerology

The timing of George H.W. Bush's New World Order speech on September 11, 1990, was no coincidence. Delivered exactly 11 years before the World Trade Center attacks on September 11, 2001, this speech signaled a shift in global dynamics—one that would culminate in catastrophic loss on American soil during the presidency of his son,

39

George W. Bush. These connections aren't mere coincidences; they reflect a deeper, occult-driven pattern that ties significant U.S. historical events together.

◆ **Why was an 11-year interval chosen between these two pivotal dates?**

The occultists behind these events didn't randomly choose a 10-year interval. Instead, they deliberately selected 11 years as a symbolic numerological period, embedding a specific timeline into U.S. history. This numerological strategy was part of a broader agenda to mark the end of the American Century and usher in the Post-American Century, where recurring loss of life would become a persistent consequence.

If you examine Table 4.1: The American 9/11 Blood Trail, you will see that the box for Bush 41's New World Order speech on September 11, 1990, shows the American flag in an upright position. This isn't because the event was pro-American but because there was no loss of life on that day. However, the bloodshed would begin exactly 11 years later, on September 11, 2001, under the watchful eye of his son, Bush 43—a tragic turning point for the nation.

◆ **How did George H.W. Bush keep these secrets hidden within the U.S. government, especially if his allegiance lay with Skull and Bones?**

The answer lies in Bush 41's strategic placement of key figures like William Casey, who served as CIA Director under the Reagan-Bush administration. Though Casey wasn't a member of Skull and Bones, he had affiliations with other secret societies, such as the Knights of Malta. Casey famously remarked, "We'll know our disinformation program is complete when everything the American people believes is false." His tenure reflected an era of secrecy and disinformation overseen by individuals deeply connected to the intelligence community.

William Casey wasn't an accidental appointment; his close ties to Prescott Bush and other prominent figures meant that he could be trusted to perpetuate disinformation and keep the truth hidden from the American public. His role in maintaining these secrets intersected with Bush 41's longstanding connections to Skull and Bones.

◆ **Could this be why rumors circulated about an attempted Reagan assassination, allegedly aimed at consolidating power within the Bush camp?**

The broader narrative reveals a disturbing pattern: the Hidden 9/11 Blood Trail weaving through American history, marked by presidential administrations that did more than keep secrets. They followed the directives of their secret societies, quietly waging war on the American people.

Slavery, "69", and the Declaration of Independence

Americans have been taught that American history is distinct from European history, with the American Revolution portrayed as a spontaneous uprising of patriotic Americans showing their rage against King George III. This view has largely stood the test of time, at least until the recent discovery of the Hidden 9/11 Blood Trail, which ties American history to European history and, even further, to the Ancient World.

In cracking the code of the New World Order, through advanced pattern matching and data analysis, these discoveries began with the uncovering of the Hidden 9/11 Blood Trail: who was hiding the bloodshed and why. This "digital forensics" revealed certain numeric patterns repeating throughout history. Among these numbers, 11, 5, and 69 stand out, acting as the fingerprints, the evidence, of a dark force slipping through humanity—murdering and hiding as it slithers.

The number 11 has many meanings, but in this context, it represents Twin Columns, a Freemasonic symbol of strength and stability. Freemasons also claim that "911" signifies an extreme challenge to strength and stability. We saw this symbolism clearly on 9/11/2001, when the Twin Towers—themselves visually representing the number 11—were attacked.

The number 5 symbolizes the Pentagon, which was also struck on 9/11. It further represents the inverted star, or pentagram, embedded in the roadways of Washington, D.C. (see Image 4.2). This pentagram hovers above the Oval Office, with its bottom tip pointing directly at the seat of American power. If we see that bottom tip as the head, it suggests the unsettling idea that the "camel's nose is under the tent."

The numbers 11 and 5 echo an old, familiar saying that holds both historical and symbolic weight: "Remember, remember, the Fifth of November." On 11/5/1605, the Gunpowder Plot unfolded as Guy Fawkes and other conspirators attempted to blow up Westminster Palace with King James I and Parliament inside. Their plan failed, and Fawkes was captured and subsequently subjected to the brutal punishment for treason: hanging, drawing, and quartering.

The number 69 is more cryptic within the Ancient and American Hidden 9/11 Blood Trails, but it is crucial because it represents slavery. This connection helps illustrate that the American 9/11 Blood Trail is merely an offshoot of the Ancient 9/11 Blood Trail, which is anchored in the destruction of the First and Second Temples of Jerusalem, as previously discussed.

Let's turn our attention to Texas, the Lone Star State, and the Emancipation Proclamation, which was signed by Abraham Lincoln on January 1, 1863, to end slavery. It took years to free the slaves in Texas, largely because the Confederates controlled the state even after the Civil War ended in April 1865. However, many people today, who celebrate Juneteenth, remain puzzled as to why it took until June 19, 1865, for the news of emancipation to reach Texas and for the slaves to be freed.

So, what delayed the Texas Rangers from delivering the news?

This is where it gets interesting... I often confuse people when I say, "They were waiting for Juneteenth."

They'll respond, "Juneteenth didn't exist yet!"

To which I reply, "Are you sure?"

The fact is, Juneteenth celebrates the day when slaves were freed in Texas. But occult numerology reveals that this date may have been chosen in advance. If you accept the idea that 69 represents slavery, then 619 (6-1-9) creates a number where the 1 acts as a dividing line between the 6 and the 9. This suggests that the date was preordained to be the day slavery would end.

So, I repeat: "The Texas Rangers were waiting for Juneteenth."

◆ **So, what does it mean that the Declaration of Independence was signed on July 4th, 1776, exactly 69 days before 9/11/1776?**

On 9/11/1776, at the Staten Island Peace Conference, Britain demanded that John Adams and Benjamin Franklin retract the Declaration of Independence, exactly 69 days after it was signed. As discussed earlier, the number 69 has significant connections to slavery. This raises questions: What invisible hand chose July 4th as the day to sign the Declaration? Did Freemasonic relationships span both the British and the Revolutionary sides? Were secret societies leaving hidden clues throughout American history, helping the 9/11 Blood Trail hide in plain sight?

While we discuss the significance of 69 and its connection to slavery, let's look at Flint, Michigan. As of 2024, 56.3% of Flint's population, or about 45,745 people, identified as Black or African American. The fact that Interstate 69 (I-69) runs through Flint, Michigan, might seem like a mere coincidence. But could the Obama Administration have singled out Flint for eco-devastation? What's behind that?

In other publications, I have revealed the obsession that Obama's handlers, including Weather Underground co-founders Bill Ayers and Bernardine Dohrn, have with Mao Zedong. Specifically, they admired Mao's essay "A Single Spark Can Start a Prairie Fire," written in January 1930. In this essay, Mao argued that even a small revolutionary movement could ignite a much larger uprising, much like a single spark can set an entire prairie on fire. A flintlock rifle needs flint to generate that first spark. The Weathermen's passion for Mao led them to publish two copies of Prairie Fire, and, metaphorically speaking, America has been on fire ever since.

The Flint water crisis began in 2014, during the Obama administration. It is regarded as one of the most significant environmental and public health disasters in recent U.S. history, with as many as 12,000 children exposed to lead-contaminated drinking water. Exposure to lead causes irreversible developmental issues, including cognitive impairments, behavioral problems, and slowed growth.

Now, go to your favorite mapping program and search for Flint, Michigan, and you'll see that Route 69 indeed runs through the city. During the era of NAFTA, which began under Bush 41 and continued through Clinton, Bush 43, and Obama, I-69 was designated as part of the planned NAFTA Superhighway, connecting the United States to Canada. Later, Trump negotiated the popular United States-Mexico-Canada Agreement (USMCA), officially replacing NAFTA. However, the broader NAFTA Superhighway project, which includes I-69, remains an ongoing infrastructure effort.

Tethering the New World to the Old

The choice of 9/11/1776 as a date anchored the American 9/11 Blood Trail to the Ancient 9/11 Blood Trail, specifically to the Battle of Vienna on 9/11/1683. The passage of exactly 93 years between 1683 and 1776 is significant. To Satanists, the number 93 represents three nines (999), as they often reverse numbers to create 666. The 9/11 Blood Trails become more embellished and robust through additional 9/11 attacks, like the 9/11 attacks in 2001, when United Airlines Flight 93 was hijacked out of Newark, New Jersey. More details will be revealed about the four flights hijacked that day, which form fingerprints suggesting deliberate actions taken years prior, preparing these flights for the 9/11 attacks of 2001.

Now that you've been introduced to the 9/11 Blood Trail, you've seen how it weaves through both American history and the Ancient World. The 20th Century was America's century, and powerful, malevolent forces preordained that there would be no loss of life on American soil on 9/11/1901. Yet they were preparing for the 21st Century, which would be marked by numerous 9/11 massacres, some already in the history books, already secretly embedded in the Hidden American 9/11 Blood Trail.

Let's now dive into Section 2, the Post-American Century, and the numerous attacks in its 24 years, as of this writing.

SECTION 2
THE POST-AMERICAN CENTURY

CHAPTER 7
GENOCIDE ART

The purpose of Section 1, The American Century, was to introduce you to the Hidden 9/11 Blood Trail and to show how it stealthily made its way from the ancient world into American history—and who benefited. This was part of how the United States was ensured major victories in both World Wars across six continents and created the greatest military on earth. The wealth generated by the greatest job-creating engine on earth—the American economy—poured vast sums of money into military research, including nuclear and rocket technologies, most of which were well beyond the reach of other countries at the time.

One of the significant 9/11 events mentioned is the laying of the keel of the U.S.S. New York, the first battleship in the U.S. Navy to host 14-inch guns, which enabled it to play a crucial role in winning World War I at sea. That date was 9/11/1911, exactly 90 years before New York City, New York State, and the United States of America were attacked. Then, on 9/11/1941, the U.S. Pentagon had its groundbreaking ceremony. To this day, the Pentagon remains the largest military headquarters in the world, covering approximately 6.5 million square feet of floor space and housing around 26,000 military and civilian employees. The Pentagon played a major role in America's achievement and maintenance of global military dominance, which persists even today.

So, who benefited the most when America was built up as it was during the 20th century, only to experience a sudden decline already underway in this century? Have you ever heard of ChinaGate and the massive military technology transfer that occurred during the Bill Clinton administration? Russia has continuously stolen and purchased vast amounts of American military technology and then cloned it. And how much did both Communist superpowers, China and Russia, benefit from Richard Nixon's invitation to partner with the U.S. in our space program? Even the Taliban was handed military dominance in the Middle East, thanks to billions of dollars' worth of state-of-the-art U.S. military equipment left behind during Biden's failed departure from Afghanistan.

The World Wars were linked in some very dark ways, as described in my other publications, but winning both World War I and World War II played a central role in making the 20th century the American Century. In short, each world war enabled the next, and World War II was critical in facilitating the approach of World War III.

Two game-changing military technologies that emerged during World War II came from the massive financial and technical commitments that only a war budget can provide: the development of the nuclear bomb by the U.S. and missile technology developed by Nazi Germany. What follows proves that a key part of the Post-American Century includes the nuclear devastation of the United States by a smaller nuclear power.

The following is an artifact—considered by some to be a work of art—called "Ominous Ikon – 1977" (Ikon with a "K"). I discovered it right in the yard of the Federal Reserve Bank in Boston, MA (Image 7.1). First, I will give you a chance to guess what you are seeing, and then I will explain it.

Image 7.1 OMINOUS IKON – 1977

Do you know what this structure represents? Is it art? I took the photo at night, so you're seeing the Boston lights through the statue. But what could this invisible shape signify? Look closely. In Image 7.2, I've filled the invisible shape with white to accentuate the contours. Do you notice a small, solid, mushroom cloud-like shape in the center, surrounded on all sides by a white cloud? Doesn't it resemble a smaller, metallic mushroom cloud, embedded within the statue? Then, do you see what looks like a much larger mushroom cloud—the white part—folding over the smaller one? What could this symbolize?

Image 7.2 OMINOUS IKON (1977) – Filled

Do you now see what looks like a larger mushroom cloud slumped over the smaller one? The fact that the larger cloud is invisible suggests it has been incinerated, right? Meanwhile, the smaller one remains intact and is solid metal. Are we supposed to imagine that the larger one was destroyed by the nuclear explosion of the smaller one? Could this larger cloud represent the United States? Do you see why I call this "Genocide Art"?

Is this America's predicted fate in the Post-American Century? Look again—do you notice that the shape of the folded-over mushroom cloud appears to symbolize America "kissing its own ass goodbye"? I do.

Does this "Genocide Art" suggest that America will be destroyed by the very technology it created?

◆ **What message is the Federal Reserve Bank sending to America with this "art"?**

According to the artist, America is not only slated to lose World War III but that powerful people in the highest offices, including those at the Federal Reserve Bank, are preparing the country for such a defeat. This sculpture and the Federal Reserve Bank are located just two miles from Logan Airport, Boston, where two flights took off from Terminal B on 9/11/2001.

We will discuss the ominous forecasting of the 9/11 attacks, hidden inside this OMINOUS IKON, later in this chapter. But for now, one last word on the pending threat from a smaller nuclear power and America's managed decline...

Obama, as president, once declared, "As the only nation ever to use nuclear weapons, the United States should continue to lead the way in eliminating them."

◆ **Who are these people?**

Isn't this the Democrat theme—that America must lead the world to peace by disarming itself first? And didn't Biden, Harris, and Milley follow a similar playbook in the failed Afghanistan withdrawal? First, they removed the soldiers, leaving behind a defenseless population. Do you remember the desperate people clinging to American planes as they fled, knowing they would likely die in the fall?

America's Enemy Within

America's decline continues to be "managed" as we enter the Post-American Century. But simply supporting MAGA—Make America Great Again—might feel good but will fail unless we also identify and bring to justice the forces waging mortal combat against America from within. These are the same groups attacking Donald Trump from all sides because he is trying to steer America away from the dangerous currents they have manipulated to control the country. They fear Trump because they fear the long arm of the law. Ultimately, it's the American people they fear—sick and tired of being sacrificed at the altar of the New World Order, which, as you now know, is the Ancient Order for the New World.

This chapter continues to introduce you to some of the "prep work" that enabled the 9/11 attacks of 2001. It serves as evidence that these attacks were indeed an "inside job." Share this information before it's too late.

Let's take a closer look at the Federal Reserve Bank in Boston, which commemorates its 1977 opening date with the Genocide Art, OMINOUS IKON (1977), as described in Image 7.1 and Image 7.2. You'll see that the building itself was foreshadowing the 9/11 attacks of 2001—more than 24 years before they occurred.

Federal Reserve Bank – Predictor of 9/11 Attacks?

I'll start by saying I visited that building, the Federal Reserve Bank in Boston, (Image 7.3), perhaps in 2007, on business. I was on one of the higher floors, possibly the 22nd or 23rd floor. As I walked to the window facing Logan Airport, I had my breath taken away by the view. It felt as though I could toss a penny and hit the runway.

You may recall that the two flights hijacked on 9/11/2001, which were flown into the Twin Towers, took off from Logan Airport. From my vantage point, I could clearly see Terminal B, where American Airlines Flight 11 and United Airlines Flight 175 began their infamous journey to New York City, culminating in the twin attacks on the World Trade Center.

My subsequent research into that mysterious building, the Federal Reserve Bank in Boston, revealed more bloody fingerprints, which complement the nuclear devastation seemingly promoted by the Genocide Art known as OMINOUS IKON (1977) (Image 7.2).

The first odd thing I noticed about that building, years ago, was the strange triangular awnings above each window. Upon closer inspection, I realized these were not awnings at all. Instead, they were solid structures, odd little triangles, as shown in Image 7.3.

Image 7.3 Obscure triangles at the Federal Reserve Bank Boston, MA

Then, I took a step back and noticed that the entire building was framed within Twin Columns, which made me even more curious. This can be seen in Image 7.4.

**Image 7.4 Twin Columns of the
Federal Reserve Bank Boston, MA**

Later, I tried to figure out the meaning behind the triangular solid window shades, and then I made a breakthrough. I realized that each side of the building had those small triangular shades, meaning that the two sides of the building were mirror images of each other. Finally, it all made sense when I realized they formed the bottom corners of a larger triangle on each floor (see Image 7.5).

The number 33 is a significant Masonic number, so what better place for the All-Seeing Eye?

Notice in Image 7.3, on the 33rd floor, there is the All-Seeing Eye, offering a spectacular yet sinister view of Logan Airport.

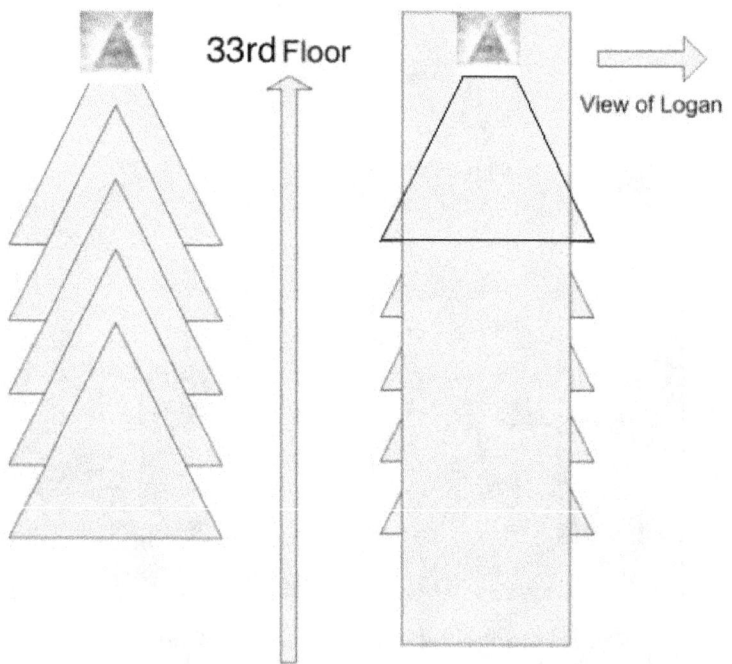

Were the liftoffs of the two flights out of Logan watched from this location on 9/11/2001?

Image 7.5 All-Seeing-Eye atop the Federal Reserve Bank Boston, MA.

Who was watching the flights lift off on 9/11/2001 from that ideal vantage point, the All-Seeing Eye? Do the American people have the right to know that critical information?

Let's wrap up with the Federal Reserve Bank in Boston by discussing the year 1977, when the building opened, and see the connection between the Genocide Art, the number "77", and possible foreknowledge of the 9/11 attacks hidden somewhere in the depths of the Federal Reserve Bank.

What about the Masonic meaning of "77"? Isn't 77 essentially two broken columns? Doesn't the number "11", which represents Twin Columns, a Freemasonic symbol of strength and stability, become 77 when each column is broken? Isn't that a corresponding Freemasonic symbol representing the lack of strength and stability? Did America lack strength and stability after the Twin Towers fell or when the Pentagon was in flames? More on the connection to the number 77...

Do you find it strange that the two American Airlines flights hijacked that day were the infamous Flight 11 (AA11), departing from Logan Airport (Boston), and the lesser-known Flight 77 (AA77), departing from Dulles Airport (Virginia)?

You are not alone in asking whether certain individuals within American Airlines had a hand in ensuring that these "sister flights," 11 and 77, were scheduled to exist and depart from the appropriate airports, anticipating their hijackings on 9/11/2001. The more you uncover about the Hidden 9/11 Blood Trail and the destruction it seems to hunger for in this Post-American Century, the more you will demand a new and thorough 9/11 Commission.

To conclude our discussion of American Airlines Flight AA77 and the possible demonic meanings associated with certain numbers, it's not about whether you or I give any weight to these bizarre numerologies; it's about whether those who hijacked the airliners do. For instance, the number 77 could symbolize twin broken columns, in contrast to twin unbroken columns like 11. Here's an interesting real-life example:

North Korean escapee Ms. Yeonmi Park grew up in the oppressive and impoverished regime of North Korea, surviving by eating rats and insects before escaping to China with her mother.

During their escape, they were separated when her mother was sold into prostitution for $65. Due to Yeonmi's youth, she was considered more valuable. In fact, she stated, "I was sold into Double-Seven" sex slavery, where high-level prostitutes served only high-dollar clients. Here, "Double-Seven" corresponds to 77.

◆ **Doesn't that sound a bit like Double-O-Seven?**

This example suggests that the Chinese may also follow Western Satanic numerology, which could have become more prominent since the Opium Wars, when British influence began to rise in Asia. These numerical associations are rooted in ancient Babylonian practices, hinting at a historical connection that transcends time and culture.

We will delve further into the four hijacked flights later in this section. But if there were indeed people within American Airlines and United Airlines ensuring that the four planes conformed to specific Masonic guidelines and numerology, there would certainly be hell to pay.

The American people are tired of being played, and if there is no statute of limitations on murder, there surely isn't one for treason.

Once again, over scripted. Once again, "too cute by half."

This introduction to Section 2 concludes with a promise: Read each chapter, right until the end of this book, and you will uncover the bloody intentions and the scale of the attacks on America. As the Hidden 9/11 Blood Trail winds through history, you will grasp how the 21st Century has been "preordained" as the "Post-American Century."

The 9/11 Blood Trail continued beyond Bush 41's era, weaving into subsequent presidencies. George W. Bush (Bush 43) presided over the events of 9/11/2001, a day that forever changed the nation and marked a dark milestone in the Post-American Century. The tragic loss of life that day was not merely a result of negligence or incompetence; it reflected a deeper, preordained agenda. Why did the occultists choose 9/11/2001 as the moment for such a catastrophic event?

The choice of 9/11/2001 as the date for the World Trade Center and Pentagon attacks was not arbitrary. As previously noted, it aligned with the 11-year gap from Bush 41's New World Order speech. This deliberate selection connected the events across decades, drawing a line through history that tied back to the ambitions of secret societies and the Deep State.

The Bush family's longstanding connections to Skull and Bones and their involvement in covert power structures allowed for the orchestration of significant global events. But the true extent of these connections would only be revealed gradually, as more details emerged about the individuals and organizations that shaped the nation's destiny from the shadows.

William Casey's disinformation strategy contributed to keeping the American public in the dark, as did the efforts of other secret society members embedded within the government. This created a web of secrecy that spanned administrations, each furthering the interests of the Deep State rather than those of the American people.

The final chapters will delve deeper into the Hidden 9/11 Blood Trail, unraveling its implications across multiple presidencies and the profound impact it has had on American society. The path forward is not only about uncovering what happened but about recognizing the patterns that continue to endanger the nation's future.

CHAPTER 8
BUSH 43 & THE GOATS

Some claim that George W. Bush (Bush 43) was the GOAT, or "Greatest of All Time," because in the remaining seven years of his two-term presidency, "there was no second 9/11 attack." However, as you will learn in this section, any subsequent 9/11 attack wasn't even scheduled until 2012—and Bush knew that.

◆ **But what exactly was Bush 43 doing in Sarasota, FL, when the planes struck the Twin Towers?**

On the morning of 9/11, Bush was reading My Pet Goat to a group of Black schoolchildren, seemingly celebrating his moment in history. If you recall from Chapter 6, in the section called "Slavery, '69,' and the Declaration of Independence," I explained how the numbers 11, 5, and 69 repeat throughout the hidden 9/11 Blood Trail and in American and world history. For the architects of 9/11, these numbers were markers, like checkboxes, embedded into history to align with ancient numerological beliefs.

◆ **So, did Bush's choice to read My Pet Goat to these children satisfy some requirement of "69" in the script of perverse numerology?**

You may be noticing that these events often seem over-scripted, as if following a hidden playbook. What then, was Bush 43 doing in Sarasota, FL, on the day before, 9/10/2001?

Of course, he was meeting with the Bin Laden family, solidifying their mutual commitment to the next day's operation. The governments of the United States and Saudi Arabia had already invested billions in preparing for these attacks, ensuring the technology and the pathways to penetrate American airspace without failure. But until we fully investigate the depths of U.S. military involvement in preparing for the attacks, we won't know how much was spent over the Clinton and Bush administrations to conceal the U.S. government's role in enabling what became the ultimate act of "domestic terrorism."

The Saudis, on the other hand, had been collaborating with the British government since the 1980s to secure an inflation-resistant financing method for acquiring advanced weaponry and technology—preparations that laid the groundwork for the 9/11 attacks. Together, they restructured British Aerospace into British Aerospace Engineering (BAE), a company that could accept up to 600,000 barrels of oil per day in exchange for military technology, allowing for long-term projects insulated from currency inflation. This partnership, known as Al-Yamamah, or "The Dove," symbolized a "peaceful" relationship that provided Saudi Arabia with a limitless supply of advanced military technology, ultimately ensuring a "successful" operation on 9/11.

The irony is chilling: the very entities behind the attacks appear to have viewed their monstrous actions as acts of "peace," believing their work on 9/11/2001 to be the culmination of this so-called "harmonious" collaboration.

The Secret Service and Getting "Tapped" by Skull & Bones?

Is it possible that the Secret Service, under oath to protect the U.S. president, was already locked down tight by a Secret Society on 9/11/2001? And haven't we more recently seen gross failures to protect President Trump during the election of 2024?

Some years ago, I met a man who had been the server for George W. Bush, Laura Bush, and four others, on 9/10/2001, the night before the 9/11 attacks of 9/11/2001. And what a story he had to tell!

An exclusive dinner was served at the Colony Beach & Tennis Resort on Longboat Key, Sarasota, which, at the time, was the most famous family tennis destination in America. It was badly damaged by hurricane Charley, three years after the event I am about to describe and was eventually torn down.

This man described that he had served an excellent dinner to the seated President of the United States, and company, and how he and another man had put their best foot forward in providing work class service to near royalty. And the evening ended with confirmation the President had been impressed.

Shortly after President Bush, Laura Bush, and the other four guests had departed, and while these two great servers were wrapping up for the night, he felt someone tap him on the shoulder. His instinct was to turn and see who was requesting his attention, at which point was told, "don't turn."

A man then said, "The President would like it very much if you would join his White House Culinary Staff and serve him at the White House. Do you accept his invitation?"

This man was new to America and knew no one in Washington D.C. where he could have lived, and said, "No." A few minutes later, his fellow server walked up and said, "You'll never guess what the Secret Service guy just said to me!"

He taps me on the shoulder, then says, "Don't turn around." He then invited me to work in the President's kitchen crew, to which the man I met asked, "what did you say?"

I said, "No, I do not know anyone in D.C. where I could live."

The first man said, "If we'd been asked together, we'd have both said Yes."

Getting "tapped", as you just learned, is the classic way to get invited into the Skull & Bones Secret Society at Yale and is how every member is recruited in their Junior Year at Yale, which includes Prescott Bush, George H.W. Bush and George W. Bush.

This story is a window into what was going on in the Bush White House in the hours before the place crashed into the Twin Towers and Pentagon, and should cause you to ask, "what else was Skull & Bones doing in the Bush Administration?"

Was Skull & Bones also in charge of the Dining Room and Staff at the White House in D.C., at that time? The Executive Office of the President? What officers of the George W. Bush Administration were also "tapped"? Did any take a blood oath? How about Chris Christie, who "got the call" from Bush on that same day, 9/10/2001, the day before the attacks on the World Trade Center Towers and Pentagon?

Chris Christie, the Twin Towers, and the 99-Year Lease

So, aside from kissing the ring of the Bin Ladens, promising to open up airspace for the Saudis Royal Family, and having two great dining room servers, "tapped", what else might George W. Bush have been doing the day before the 9/11 attacks?

◆ **Was Bush wrapping up his "pre-9/11 office work?"**

If you think about it, it cannot be easy to maintain a schedule in the Oval Office with key figures dropping by unannounced and throwing curve balls into the calendar. And having a conversation completely off the record may be hard to accomplish from the Oval Office as well.

So, whatever the reason, George W. Bush gave Chris Christie a ring that day and asked him if he would become the United States Attorney for the District of New Jersey, which he clearly accepted. Christie served in that role from January 17, 2002 until December 1, 2008. But, why might Christie have been on the mind of Bush on that fate filled day, just before the Twin Towers were scheduled to come down?

◆ **Did you know? In the days leading up to the September 11, 2001 attacks, there was notable trading activity involving United Airlines and American Airlines stocks.**

Specifically, an unusually high volume of put options—financial instruments that increase in value when a stock's price declines—were purchased for these airlines.

"Buy low, sell high" is always on the mind of every investor. So, what kind of "inside information" would be useful if someone knew the Twin Towers were coming down? The strategy seems obvious: buy the real estate, increase the insurance coverage, and prepare to rebuild modern replacements on the property from scratch. With this in mind, let's examine what might have resulted from that conversation between Bush and Christie on 9/10/2001, where insurance payouts were undoubtedly a topic of interest.

Fifty days before the World Trade Center was destroyed, Larry Silverstein—developer and owner of the infamous Building 7—signed a 99-year lease on the entire World Trade Center complex. He increased the insurance, including coverage for terrorist attacks, and subsequently received over $4.5 billion from insurance companies after the tragedy.

World Trade Center Building 7 (WTC 7) housed offices for several U.S. government agencies, including the Central Intelligence Agency (CIA), the Secret Service, and the Securities and Exchange Commission (SEC). Silverstein Properties, led by Larry Silverstein, acquired this 99-year lease on the WTC complex from the Port Authority of New York and New Jersey. Clearly, Silverstein emerged as the winner in this deal.

But, for every winner, there's a loser. In this case, the taxpayers of New York and New Jersey bore the loss. Wasn't it the job of the United States Attorney for the District of New Jersey to investigate this? Did Chris Christie, in his role, ever look into the unusually high volume of put options on the stocks of American and United Airlines? Or was Christie appointed by Bush to ensure that no one in the media ever dared to use the words "INSURANCE FRAUD"?

It is not anti-Sematic to state that Larry Silverstein appears to have gotten away with the most classic name form of insurance fraud, Jewish Lighting.

Hurricane Charley, Dick Cheney, Cleaning Up the Evidence

A few years after the infamous "9/11 Attack Eve Dinner" at the Colony Beach & Tennis Resort near Sarasota, Florida, this popular destination for tennis enthusiasts was struck by three hurricanes—Charley and Frances in 2004, and Wilma in 2005—causing significant damage. "The Colony" eventually closed in 2010 and was demolished in 2018.

I mention these hurricanes to introduce a term I first heard following the devastation of Hurricane Katrina, a term used by people who began to believe in weather manipulation: the "Dick Cheney Hurricane Machine." And they were serious.

At the time, I thought it was some kind of joke. But as I'll explain in later chapters, there came a point when I stopped considering it funny. Along the way, I discovered a few "curious fingerprints" linking the New World Order to Hurricane Katrina and, quite possibly, to the Hidden 9/11 Blood Trail.

One of the most memorable images of Hurricane Katrina's aftermath is then-President George W. Bush taking an aerial tour of Louisiana, Mississippi, and Alabama—the three states most severely impacted by the storm—instead of visiting the disaster zones on the ground. Many viewed this as a lack of engagement with those affected by the disaster, and some echoed Kanye West's famous words, "George Bush doesn't care about Black people."

If you recall from the section titled "The Hidden Symbolism of the Numbers 11, 5, and 69," these numbers repeat throughout 9/11-related events in history. Hurricane Katrina appears to share this numerical symbolism.

"K" is the 11th letter of the alphabet, meaning Katrina was the 11th named storm of the season. Each hurricane season begins with "A" and increments by letter for each storm. Katrina caused $125 billion in damages, led to catastrophic levee failures, and claimed over 1,800 lives. The year was 2005.

This pattern of 11 and 5 appears repeatedly in significant events. Additionally, the number 69, which you've seen associated with Juneteenth, symbolizing "slavery," may have influenced the selection of New Orleans as Katrina's target, if we consider the storm as a possible act of weather warfare.

Is this why Bush opted for a "fly-over"? Were his actions intended to symbolize harm toward Black communities? Once you delve into the possibilities of weather manipulation, you'll see that Category 5 storms can indeed be created—and they can be directed toward specific targets, like New Orleans.

So, I no longer laugh when I hear the term "Dick Cheney's Hurricane Machine." If I uncover a few more "fingerprints" linking Katrina to these patterns, I would consider formally adding Hurricane Katrina to the Hidden 9/11 Blood Trail, based on the recurring presence of 11, 5, and 69.

9/11 Rabbit Holes: Woolworth Building Missile Attack

Years ago, while researching Boston's Custom House, I uncovered connections to certain dark architectural patterns hiding in plain sight. (See Image 8.1) This will be explored further in a later installment of this book series, The Hidden 9/11 Blood Trail. The land for the Custom House was originally purchased by President Andrew Jackson, a prominent Freemason and one of the key founders of the Democratic Party. If the Custom House seems to resemble an "all-seeing-eye," that's because it was designed with such symbolism in mind.

Image 8.1 Boston's Custom House

The question, "Where is it looking?" will be answered in a future edition. There is indeed a 9/11 connection that suggests foreknowledge of the 9/11 flights departing from Logan Airport in Boston. I've included this image (Image 8.1) to emphasize the resemblance between the Boston Custom House, London's Big Ben, and the Woolworth Building in New York City—two structures with groundbreaking dates later than Boston's Custom House.

My research into the Woolworth Building in NYC revealed that, at its groundbreaking on November 4, 1910, it was positioned to appear, from certain angles, as though it were located between the two future Twin Towers of the World Trade Center. In historical photos, the Twin Towers appear almost as two legs, with the

Woolworth Building positioned in between, symbolically like a phallus. And on 9/11/2001, that "phallus" appears to have produced a deadly ejaculation—right on schedule.

On the morning of 9/11, reports emerged from people throughout New York City who called into radio and TV stations claiming they saw missiles being fired from the Woolworth Building. Early media coverage included these claims before they were censored by federal authorities. There remains audio and video of explosions, clearly unrelated to the collapse of the Twin Towers, as well as eye-witness testimony from New Yorkers and journalists.

To find more: Google "9/11 Rabbit Holes: Woolworth Building Missile" to locate video footage.

Watch the first 2 minutes and 48 seconds of the video, where you can reportedly see missiles being launched from the Woolworth Building—missiles that may have even struck the World Trade Center. The Woolworth Building housed the headquarters of Telex Corporation, later acquired by Halliburton, the company associated with former Vice President Dick Cheney. While this is not proof that Telex, Halliburton, or Dick Cheney orchestrated missile launches on 9/11, it raises disturbing questions that demand answers—answers that both Dick and Liz Cheney must be compelled to provide under oath, and polygraph.

If any of these connections prove true, we could be looking at charges of treason against Dick Cheney and Liz Cheney for actions that go beyond mere political maneuvering. Consider the implications:

If missiles were indeed launched from the Woolworth Building on 9/11, that would implicate Cheney in a plot of unfathomable betrayal against the American people;

If the so-called "Dick Cheney Hurricane Machine" was used to weaponize weather against American citizens, this would amount to a war on the homeland, by its own leaders;

And if the Cheneys have had a hand in orchestrating the relentless persecution of thousands of Americans—Americans who, after January 6th, were locked away in solitary confinement for months, held in facilities better suited for Communist Russia than the United States—then they have crossed a line that places them firmly in the realm of treason.

These detainees, held under the pretense of justice, are victims of a Kangaroo Court system that the Cheneys seem all too willing to endorse—a system that has stripped away their Constitutional rights, thrown them into gulag-like cells, and effectively silenced them. The January 6th detainees are being made examples of, held as political prisoners in their own country, their very existence as prisoners of conscience a stain on the American promise of freedom.

If any of these "connections" are proven, then Dick Cheney and Liz Cheney should indeed be brought to account on the gravest of charges: treason against the American people. Our nation cannot allow those who claim to serve it to wield power in a way that betrays the very foundations on which it stands.

CHAPTER 9
BENGHAZI – ANOTHER INSIDE JOB

It is often rumored that before a member of a secret society is sworn in as President, he must first take a blood oath, pledging loyalty—under pain of death—to that society or some other dark force. It's not difficult to imagine both Bush 41 and Bush 43 doing just that, perhaps through Skull & Bones, giving "Bonesmen" an exceptional level of influence. This influence might explain the events that unfolded after dinner on 9/10/2001, at The Colony. Or perhaps their allegiance is to the New World Order, like the one George H.W. Bush bragged about on 9/11/1990.

So, did Bush 43 demand a similar oath from Obama before relinquishing his grip on the White House? If so, blood or no blood, I have a strong sense of the dark obligation Obama may have sworn to uphold—a revelation I will share at the end of this chapter.

If Obama had indeed taken a blood oath before his public oath to become president, it would not have been his first encounter with secrecy.

As we explore Obama's background more closely, a complex picture begins to emerge, one that suggests his rise to the presidency may have been orchestrated long before he set foot on the political stage. Journalist and investigative author Wayne Madsen delves deeply into this hidden narrative in his book, The Manufacturing of a President: The CIA's Insertion of Barack H. Obama Jr. into the White House. Madsen contends that Obama's ascent was not simply a product of ambition or talent, but rather a carefully designed trajectory crafted within the heart of America's intelligence apparatus.

Madsen writes, "...Obama was groomed from an early age to be a 'Manchurian candidate,' prepared to step into the White House when the time was right." In Obama's case, "Manchuria" was located not in a foreign land, but in the secretive corridors of the CIA headquarters in Langley, Virginia.

Madsen's work sheds light on Obama's connections to key figures and institutions linked to U.S. intelligence, raising questions about the true nature of his early influences and motivations. This perspective challenges the familiar narrative of Obama as a self-made man, suggesting instead that his path may have been shaped by powerful interests within the intelligence community. As if to underscore his complex relationship with power, Obama reportedly told senior aides in 2011, "Turns out I'm really good at killing people. Didn't know that was gonna be a strong suit of mine," referring to the extensive use of drone strikes during his presidency. His administration authorized 542 drone strikes, resulting in an estimated 3,797 deaths, including 324 civilians.

What follows in this chapter takes a closer look at the troubling evidence surrounding the Benghazi attack—a tragedy that I believe was not merely a random act of violence against American interests in the Middle East, but an orchestrated event with the hallmarks of a 9/11-style assault on American soil, with high-level involvement from the U.S. government. Occurring on the 11th anniversary of the 9/11/2001 attacks, the Benghazi assault appears as a deliberate act, strategically timed to align with what I call the "Hidden 9/11 Blood Trail." Furthermore, it happened exactly 22 years after George H.W. Bush's infamous "New World Order" speech to Congress.

When people hear the name "Benghazi," they often think of then-Secretary of State Hillary Clinton and her highly visible role in the aftermath, including her use of BleachBit to erase 33,000 emails already under subpoena. As you'll see in this chapter—and throughout this book—this was only the beginning. Her actions went far beyond violations of the Federal Records Act (FRA), perjury, and false statements (18 U.S. Code § 1001). It was as if these visible transgressions were designed to be a bright, shiny distraction for Republicans to pursue, all the while knowing that the statute of limitations would erode any real chance of repercussions.

◆ **Meanwhile, the question remains: how do we bring Hillary to justice for her real crimes in Benghazi, Libya?**

That's simple. Pursue her for the Benghazi crimes with no statute of limitations: the murder of Americans. But the guilty party extends far beyond Hillary Clinton alone. Those responsible include key figures from the entire Obama administration, including Joe Biden, as well as others who will be named later in this chapter.

After receiving an initial briefing about the attack on September 11, 2012, Obama demonstrated a disturbing lack of concern for the lives of Americans suddenly placed in harm's way. Instead of staying actively engaged, he delegated responsibility to his national security team and failed to order an immediate military response from nearby bases in Italy or other locations, despite urgent pleas for help. Unlike his presence in the Situation Room during the raid on Osama bin Laden's compound, Obama chose not to oversee operations related to Benghazi.

To make matters worse for the 36 Americans trapped inside the U.S. Consulate, a stand-down order was reportedly in place, preventing any response from the Army, Air Force, Navy, and Marines. This included blocking the deployment of urgent help stationed at the CIA annex just 1 mile away.

Who could have orchestrated such a stand-down order involving both U.S. military and intelligence assets? Could this be the evidence that high-ranking officials like Mark Milley, Hillary Clinton, and others were part of a scheme to maximize the death toll?

As depicted in the movie 13 Hours: The Secret Soldiers of Benghazi, or and through other accounts, we know there were five heroic men who defied the stand-down order, risking their lives to save others. Tyrone Woods, Glen Doherty, Mark Geist, John Tiegen, and Kris Paronto fought courageously; Woods and Doherty ultimately sacrificed their lives, while Tiegen sustained severe injuries.

Hillary Clinton faced widespread criticism for leaving the consulate vulnerable to attack by reportedly rejecting up to 650 requests for additional security from Ambassador J. Christopher Stevens, one of the four Americans killed in the September 11, 2012, attack. His body, along with those of Sean Smith, Glen Doherty, and Tyrone Woods, was returned on a C-17 to Joint Base Andrews in Maryland. There, President Obama, Hillary Clinton, and other officials met with the families of the fallen—a scene for which Hillary later received substantial criticism.

Could it have been her intention that day to witness the offloading of more caskets, perhaps even 36? Was this connected to the controversial stand-down order? Could it have been an attempt to maximize American casualties? Such questions arise when considering the actions of those who could willingly orchestrate or fail to prevent harm to Americans.

Some accounts from family members of the victims have indicated that Hillary Clinton's private remarks differed from her public statements. According to Pat Smith, mother of Sean Smith, and Charles Woods, father of Tyrone Woods, Clinton allegedly attributed the attack to the anti-Islam video Innocence of Muslims, which they later felt was misleading.

Yes, Innocence of Muslims was blamed by Hillary Clinton, Obama, Biden, Susan Rice, Valerie Jarrett, Eric Holder, John Kerry, and many others. But was this just a straw man argument? This low-budget, inflammatory movie trailer, produced in America, became the official explanation for the Benghazi attack—a convenient answer to deflect deeper questions about motive.

Now that you know it was a pre-planned 9/11 attack, strategically timed to stain American history and perfectly aligned with the aims of the New World Order, are you more curious about that poorly made movie trailer?

The video that Clinton and others initially cited as the cause of the 2012 Benghazi attack was a low-budget, controversial film produced in the United States. It depicted the Prophet Muhammad in a negative light, sparking protests across parts of the Middle East and North Africa. Yet, it was produced without any intention of theatrical release or educational purpose. At just 14 minutes, it appeared to serve a single purpose: to incite anger and attract attention. So, was that its intended audience?

Was the Obama administration involved in creating this inflammatory video and ensuring its release to the Middle East in early September, just in time to set the stage for the 9/11 attack in Benghazi?

Is it now becoming clear that Benghazi was an inside job, and the video Innocence of Muslims was merely part of a coverup, a straw man to mask the true motives behind the attack?

Did Obama "save the date"—9/11/2012—at the beginning of his first term on January 20, 2009, prioritizing the preparations and coverup for the pending assault? Was the Benghazi attack, hidden from the public as a "reaction" to a video, the defining moment of Obama's presidency, ensuring his allegiance to the aims of Skull and Bones or similar secretive forces?

And did he select Hillary Clinton as Secretary of State from day one, trusting her skill in concocting diversions and standing firm behind a straw man?

Is there a single individual involved in this plot who has not committed treason? Has the time come to utilize polygraph testing for traitors—a method far more humane than waterboarding?

Now that you see why Benghazi is an official part of the Hidden 9/11 Blood Trail, we can examine how these same forces, deeply embedded within the U.S. government, have schemed to add further attacks to that Blood Trail, ensuring the 21st Century unfolds as the Post-American Century.

Let's proceed to uncover how this hidden attack on U.S. soil links to further tragedies, weaving a trail of blood that stretches from modern American history back to the Ancient World.

CHAPTER 10
WEATHER WARFARE ON THE U.S.A.

I have been researching 9/11 attacks, 9/11 events and 9/11 architecture, for years, which first revealed to me that a clear 9/11 Blood Trail in fact existed. Then, I began to follow the blood stains to learn about the real history of the United States, the hidden history of the United States, and how our 9/11 history is inexorably tied to the 9/11 history of the world, including the Ancient World. This is when I realized that bloody history was, "hiding in plain sight."

Chapter 3 and Chapter 4 as well as Tables 3.1 and 4.1 detail many 9/11 events and 9/11 attacks throughout world history and U.S. history. In the process of reading this book, hopefully you have come to understand how the American 9/11 Blood Trail revealed the concepts and terms which are surely new to you, the pre-ordained American Century (Section 1) and the pre-ordained Post-American Century (Section 2).

As my understanding grew, I came to see the Post-American Century as a downhill process, meaning it is only slated to get worse, with an accelerated decline, like a ball rolling down a hill, so long as the Deep State is still secretly calling the shots. Never think in terms of steady state, or that the worst is behind us, because the rate of decline for America is already slated to go accelerate.

This came to me when I realized what neither the "Mainstream Media" nor Conservative Talk Radio ever mentioned that the Benghazi attack was in fact a 9/11 attack, keeping it on the "Hidden" 9/11 Blood trail. This critical omission was accomplished, in part, with that "false flag" the Obama Administration had arranged, that a video was the cause of that attack, a video which they appear to have made. Once I needed to decide whether or not to seriously consider adding it to the 9/11 Blood Trail, I checked to see if it conformed to the requirement of loss of life for Americans, which it did. Lastly, that loss of life needed to be on American soil, in order to qualify. So, when I confirmed that under international law, U.S. embassies and consulates are the foreign installations most closely treated as American soil, I knew I was on to something big.

Once I determined that the Benghazi attack wasn't a response to a video but a direct assault on America and its influence in the region, I knew it was a crucial addition to the 9/11 Blood Trail. Analyzing the role the video played for the administration as a "straw man argument" – and Hillary's subsequent cover-ups – solidified Benghazi's place on the "Hidden" 9/11 Blood Trail. Today, most have forgotten that Benghazi even occurred on a 9/11 anniversary, which seems intentional by design.

The Obama Administration orchestrated a 9/11 attack on America, ensured the "success" of the attack from the highest levels of government, then "succeeded" again, by keeping it hidden from the American public. For those demanding Obama's allegiance – perhaps even a "blood oath" upon his swearing-in – Benghazi may have been his greatest "accomplishment." The transition from the George W. Bush Administration on January 20, 2009, could then be seen as a complete success, from the perspective of Skull and Bones, the Yale Secret Society of which George W. Bush was a member.

Years after 9/11/2012, I came to recognize Benghazi as yet another "inside job," a "false flag" like other attacks along the Hidden 9/11 Blood Trail. This realization brought me to see a disturbing pattern. The architects of this blood trail are ruthless and relentless, always planning the next assault, always taking great strides to keep it a secret. Given my familiarity with the numbers 11, 5, and 69, I sensed we were due for a "celebration" of Benghazi's, a 5-year anniversary, as it were. So, on my calendar, I marked a bright red X on 9/11/2017!

The Countdown to 9/11/2017

In 2016, when I discovered that the next 9/11 attack on America was scheduled for 2017, I knew this wasn't just a theory—it was a fact. I quickly set to work, determined to warn people and, hopefully, prevent it. Initially, I started by spreading the word personally.

On September 10, 2016, I was at a campaign rally in Littleton, MA, where I overheard a woman say to another, "Tomorrow's 9/11." I couldn't help but interrupt, saying, "There won't be an attack tomorrow, because it's only 2016. The next attack isn't scheduled until 2017." Unsurprisingly, they seemed skeptical.

Later, I found someone with a video recorder and asked him to record me. In that video, I made two key predictions: first, that there would be no 9/11 attack the next day because it was only 2016; and second, that the next planned 9/11 attack was set for 2017. I also displayed early versions of the Hidden 9/11 Blood Trail, specifically Table 4.1, indicating the progression of attacks and the projected date for the next one on 9/11/2017.

You can see that video on my YouTube channel, @psyopwars11. It's about three minutes long and explains the reasoning behind my prediction. I talk about the 9/11 Blood Trail as it stood in 2016, mentioning how Benghazi was the 11-year anniversary massacre in "celebration" of the 9/11/2001 attacks.

In my video, you can see the numerous Trump/Pence signs in the background, validating my claim that it was recorded on September 10, 2016. My prediction that there would be no 9/11 attack the next day proved accurate, as history confirmed. I went a step further, forecasting that the next planned 9/11 attack would occur the following year, in 2017, on the 5-year commemoration of the Benghazi attack on the U.S. consulate on 9/11/2012. This led me to 2017: a calculation of $2001 + 11 + 5$.

Get the Word Out

I was absolutely convinced an attack was imminent, and with only one year to spread the message, I set to work. I launched a website called Stop911.com, where I posted my video from Littleton, along with additional videos and articles, hoping to alert others to the looming threat we faced yet again.

Reaching people proved challenging; few were interested in exploring the historical background essential to understanding my revelations about the 9/11 Blood Trail. To bridge this gap, I designed a 52-card game called Target USA, intended to make learning engaging while revealing the historical layers of the 9/11 Blood Trail through gameplay.

Target USA highlighted America's longstanding presence in the crosshairs of the British Royals, linked to the occult significance of 9/11. My primary aim with the game was to foster unity, hoping to bring together families that had been torn apart by political divides. (See Image 11.1)

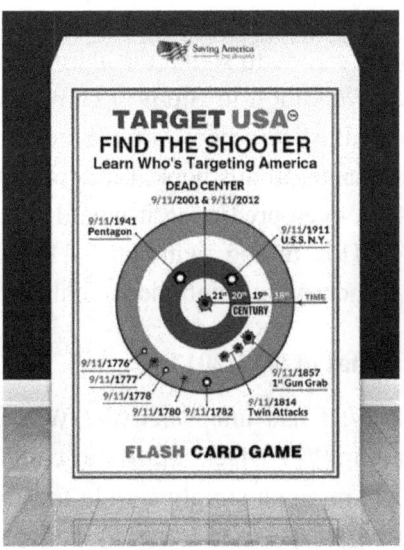

Image 11.1 Target USA – 52-Card Educational Playing Deck

During the 2016 presidential election, it wasn't uncommon to hear stories of political divisions even within families. Some couples faced exchanges like this: the husband might say, "I'm voting for Trump!" to which the wife would respond, "If you vote for Trump, I want a divorce!" The husband's reply? "If you vote for Hillary, I'm moving to Canada!"

The goal of Target USA was to bring unity by offering a shared understanding of the true forces dividing America. When the truth about those behind the 9/11 attacks becomes known, that knowledge can help foster unity by removing the source of manufactured division—one family at a time.

On the subject of national unity, I delve into this theme further in my other book, The Camelot Murders and the Crucifixion of Mary Jo. Chapter 1, National Unity in the Crosshairs, introduces the concept that evidence exists to show that all the deaths surrounding JFK's Camelot were indeed murders. This book reveals how the downfall of Camelot was a covert Deep State assault on Christianity, Catholicism, and American unity, a sinister campaign that has succeeded—until now.

Returning to my efforts to sound the alarm about the impending 9/11/2017 attack: in addition to Stop911.com and the Target USA card game, I also published a book titled Fortress Harvard – Think Tank for Royal Revenge. In this book, I reiterated the warning of an attack on 9/11/2017, even predicting it would occur between 7 AM and 11 AM EST. This timing, with its 7-11 pattern, mirrors the significance of 9-11, carrying symbolic weight in the occult.

The Where and What of 9/11/2017

By August 2017, I had uncovered the When, Why, and Who behind the impending 9/11 attack, but I still couldn't determine the Where or What. My research simply couldn't reveal those specifics. Understanding the urgency of spreading my findings, though, a friend suggested I tune into Alex Jones's radio show and consider calling in.

When I turned on the radio, I heard Alex's guest, Pastor Rodney Howard-Browne from South Africa, discussing serious topics: public threats against President Trump, Satanists embedded within the shadow government, and the forces of darkness at play. Listening to him speak, I became convinced that Pastor Howard-Browne, with his profound insights and unwavering Christian ministry, would understand my prediction about the looming 9/11 attack. I made urgent plans to travel to Florida to meet him, arriving at his Tampa Bay Church, The River, by the following morning.

I requested a meeting with Pastor Howard-Browne, explaining that I had come to Florida urgently to discuss an impending 9/11 attack on America. I even handed him a copy of my book, Fortress Harvard – Think Tank for Royal Revenge, for immediate review. Unfortunately, I never had the opportunity to meet with him or discuss my research. It became clear that he didn't believe me. I felt certain of this during his Sunday service at the River Church, where I attended in hopes of connecting. During his sermon, he mentioned, "We're only a few weeks away from the 16th anniversary of 9/11. Not much going on there…"

As I sat in the pews, I was internally screaming, "It's the 5th anniversary of Benghazi, which is the 11th anniversary of 9/11/2001!" But no one heard me—not even those who could be directly in harm's way.

Fast Forward to 9/11/2017

Historically, I had been skeptical about the possibility of weather manipulation, despite years of rumors and talk, including references to "Dick Cheney's Hurricane Machine." But the events of the morning of 9/11/2017 soon changed my perspective.

On August 25th, a few weeks prior, Hurricane Harvey devastated Houston, Texas, after stalling offshore and intensifying into a Category 5 hurricane. When a hurricane stops over warm water, it gains strength, and Harvey seemed to pause, almost as if it were eyeing its target, before moving in to unleash destruction. To me, it looked like a calculated strike—like a King Cobra preparing to attack.

On the morning of September 11, 2017, I was deeply concerned about Hurricane Irma, which had entered the Gulf of Mexico. Irma seemed "confused" about its path, once again pausing while it gained strength. At that point, it was a Category 3 hurricane with sustained winds around 115 mph. The storm had already devastated the Caribbean and Key West as a Category 5 hurricane with winds reaching 185 mph but was now stalled in the Gulf.

Then, as if controlled by a joystick, Hurricane Irma went from stationary to rapidly moving. At 7 AM EST—exactly the time I had predicted the attack would begin—Irma made landfall in Tampa, Florida. And where did it strike? Directly at Pastor Howard-Browne's River Church, where I had previously traveled to meet him. The storm caused minimal damage to his church but managed to topple a historic church tower nearby.

Irma then continued east into central Florida, before taking a sharp 90-degree left turn north, almost as though it were following a pre-determined path. It raced through the middle of Florida, crossing into Georgia by 11 AM, precisely on schedule. I noted that 7 and 11 formed another Masonic numeric pattern, similar to the two flights out of Logan on 9/11/2001, which took off around 7 AM. Later, on that ill-fated day, at 11 AM, New York City Mayor Rudy Giuliani ordered the evacuation of Lower Manhattan south of Canal Street, after the Twin Towers had collapsed.

In my book, I discuss these events alongside a video I recorded on September 10, 2016, and my predictions. My research, forecasts, and presence in Tampa prior to the attack combined to reveal the What, Why, Who, Where, and When of an impending attack on the United States—an event that ultimately resulted in 134 deaths and approximately $77 billion in damages.

I was quickly becoming convinced of weather manipulation, but when Hurricane Irma fit seamlessly into the 9/11 Blood Trail, I began to believe in something far more sinister: Weather Warfare. Add a

Satanic undertone, and the whole picture becomes easier to see. The trio of hurricanes—Harvey, Irma, and Maria—spell "H.I.M.," a reference to Lucifer. These named storms, seemingly chosen by those with power over life and death, suggest that the same people who direct devastation can also cause storms to fade away at will. The storms are alphabetical, and there were three between Irma and Maria: H, I, J, K, L, and M.

In 2017, Storm J was named Jose, following Irma. I vividly recall how Jose snaked up the East Coast, causing no significant damage, then hovered off New York City for approximately four to five days, from September 18 or 19 until September 22, 2017. It felt like an eternity. As I watched weather reports on TV, I noticed that each update showed the storm's spiraling shape forming the number 69 repeatedly. The pattern of 69 is a key part of the 9/11 pattern, which also includes 11 and 5, as I've previously discussed. It certainly seemed contrived, almost like a clear warning aimed at New York City, which had already been in the bloody crosshairs on 9/11/2001.

All three hurricanes reached Category 5 strength at some point. What are the odds of that? This trio, centered around Hurricane Irma on September 11, 2017, marked the five-year "commemoration" of the Benghazi massacre. This so-called commemoration, symbolized by a staggering death toll of 3,259 and destruction totaling approximately $266.6 billion, underscores a 5-5-5 tribute to the horrors of Benghazi. It's a demonstration of the deadly reach of those who manipulate the weather—a reach that, as you'll see, extends much further in this book.

Finally, when you recognize the disturbing possibility that these four hurricanes were orchestrated by people who hold a deep hatred for America, you may also realize that the Benghazi massacre was, in a sense, an "inside job." Benghazi connects these storms to the 9/11 Blood Trail, reinforcing the reality that it plays a crucial yet hidden role on the Hidden 9/11 Blood Trail.

This chapter concludes with my firm stance on Weather Warfare and why I consider some of these so-called "Geo Engineers," who manipulate the weather, to be epic traitors against the United States. If you still doubt this, read on.

CHAPTER 11
VIETNAM, WEATHER WARFARE & THE USSR

Shortly after Hurricanes Harvey, Irma, and Maria struck, I realized that Weather Warfare might not be just a concept but a reality we're already facing. My initial research introduced me to many phenomena that first-time investigators often encounter: aerosol spraying from planes, unusual droughts, and the massive HAARP facility in Alaska, known as the High-Frequency Active Auroral Research Program. My conviction grew stronger when I found GeoEngineeringWatch.org—a groundbreaking website dedicated to this topic, backed by scientific research.

For example, Dane Wigington, lead researcher and administrator of GeoEngineeringWatch.org, has devoted over two decades to exposing covert global climate engineering operations. With a background in solar energy and previous experience at Bechtel Power Corporation, Wigington has extensively studied the environmental and health impacts of geoengineering. His research delves into the effects of atmospheric aerosol spraying and ionospheric heaters, such as HAARP, on Earth's climate systems. Wigington's documentary The Dimming aims to raise public awareness about the realities of climate engineering that often go unnoticed.

Recently, Wigington's articles have highlighted how microwave energy might be used to keep hurricanes offshore, potentially strengthening them before landfall. He noted several hurricanes approaching the mid-Atlantic states, particularly near North Carolina, that may have been influenced by such techniques. His research suggests that microwave energy, possibly directed from land, can narrow and intensify a storm's bands, keeping it offshore until it reaches a desired strength. Once intensified, this interference can be halted, allowing the storm to move inland. Additionally, microwaves might slow a storm at landfall, amplifying water damage.

Three major hurricanes impacting the Eastern Seaboard—Florence (2018), Dorian (2019), and Matthew (2016)—claimed 91 lives in the U.S. and caused $39.1 billion in damages. It's possible that one or more of these storms were manipulated. If anyone has tracked such activity, it's Dane Wigington, who monitors various facilities in affected areas, such as:

A Doppler radar station (NEXRAD) near Raleigh, NC

Research Triangle Park (RTP), a major research center where some companies and university labs study atmospheric science

Fort Bragg and Seymour Johnson Air Force Base, both of which may have microwave communication facilities used for radar and other purposes.

Through his ongoing investigations, Wigington continues to shed light on the hidden world of climate manipulation, raising questions about the potential role of Weather Warfare in recent disasters.

◆ **How long was this weather warfare going on?**

Make Mud Not War

My research into weather warfare led me back to the Vietnam War and a then top-secret program known as Operation Popeye. While B-52 bombers targeted sections of the Ho Chi Minh Trail across Laos, Cambodia, and Vietnam, they had limited success in stopping supply routes, as much of the enemy's equipment was moved by bicycle, with some bikes carrying loads of up to 200 pounds. To counter this, the U.S. military decided to "Make Mud Not War"—deploying cloud-seeding technology to make the jungle trails impassable.

Operation Popeye aimed to extend the monsoon season over specific areas of the Ho Chi Minh Trail, disrupting enemy supplies and movement. Reports vary on the exact number of sorties flown, but around 15,000 cloud-seeding flights were conducted from 1967 to 1972 to carry out the operation. This marked a significant commitment to weather manipulation by the U.S. Department of Defense.

The expertise gained during the Vietnam War with cloud seeding formed just one part of the technologies that, today, might enable full weather control—potentially even manufacturing hurricanes. Now, weather manipulation involves an array of advanced techniques, including Solar Radiation Management, Stratospheric Aerosol Injection, Ionospheric Heaters, Microwave Radiation Systems, Laser-Based Atmospheric Heating, Ocean Surface Modification, Artificial Upwelling and Downwelling Devices, and Directed Energy Systems, among others.

In early October 2024, Dane Wigington—founder of GeoEngineeringWatch.org—briefed state representatives and senators from North and South Carolina on these weather modification technologies. In his discussions, he outlined the potential influence of such technologies on weather patterns, including hurricanes like Helene and Milton. But there is still much more to uncover.

◆ **How much longer will Americans tolerate the hidden forces behind Weather Warfare?**

Trumparilla in the Crosshairs?

On September 28, 2022, Hurricane Ian slammed into Fort Myers, Florida, with devastating force. A Category 4 storm with sustained winds of 150 mph, it was labeled a "500-year storm"—an event so catastrophic that the region had no historical record of anything comparable.

Just a year earlier, the vibrant harbor of Fort Myers hosted a pro-Trump event called Trumparilla. I had visited this same harbor, struck by its energy and beauty. Little did I realize I was standing on ground destined to become the epicenter of Ian's wrath. It's hard not to wonder: could this devastation have been by design? Was Fort Myers targeted through geoengineering under the Biden Administration, delivering a symbolic—and literal—blow to a pro-Trump stronghold?

As always, the narrative shifted immediately to "global warming."

Fast forward to the administration's cold and dismissive responses to the victims of Hurricanes Helene and Milton, and a darker picture begins to emerge. The idea that Weather Warfare might be used against Americans no longer seems unthinkable. In the next chapter, we'll delve into the disturbing evidence that those orchestrating mass destruction don't just evade accountability—they celebrate their success.

But before that, consider the chilling words of William Casey, former CIA Director under Reagan and Bush:

"We'll know our disinformation program is complete when everything the American people believes is false."

This calculated deception has paved the way for the Green New Deal—a grand lie built on the foundation of manipulated climate narratives.

Reflect, too, on President Ronald Reagan's iconic challenge at the Berlin Wall in 1987:

"Mr. Gorbachev, tear down this wall!"

At the time, Mikhail Gorbachev was leading the Soviet Union. Two years later, the wall fell, marking the end of the USSR. When a reporter asked the newly "unemployed" Gorbachev what he planned to do next, his response was simple but ominous:

"I'm going Green."

◆ *Isn't "Green" just the new Red?*

CHAPTER 12
ROUTE "91" HARVEST FEST MASSACRE

The Route "91" Harvest Fest Massacre was the largest mass shooting in modern American history, yet seems to be slipping into the "forgotten history" category, as there has been a complete lack of new information. So, this chapter concludes Section 2, entitled the "Post-American Century," and the book entitled "The Hidden 9/11 Blood Trail - Weather Warfare & the Bloody Jackpot in Vegas," which presents the very first motive for the shooter and the bloodbath he masterminded and carried out.

Some Americans still remember, there was a deadly massacre in Las Vegas, at 10:05 PM on October 1, 2017, which lasted 10 minutes. 58 people were killed on the night of the attack, with two more succumbing to their injuries. Over 850 people were injured in total, with about 400 of these injuries directly resulting from gunfire.

Stephen Paddock brought 23 firearms into his hotel suite on the 32nd floor of the Mandalay Bay Hotel, and fired down into the crowd below, where around 22,000 concertgoers were attending the Route 91 Harvest music festival. Panic and pandemonium ensued, as people lay wounded and dying in the arms of loved ones. Paddock was found deceased from a self-inflicted gunshot wound when police entered his hotel room at 11:20 PM, ending the horror for many, but starting the misery for many others.

Once again, America has fallen into the familiar trap of the so-called "lone gunman," as the phrase "he acted alone" is repeated ad infinitum. Meanwhile, public disclosure of videos from the moments leading up to the massacre remains extremely limited, and the investigation into the shooter's motive has run cold. Yet, as you uncover its connection to the Hidden 9/11 Blood Trail, you'll see that the search for a motive has not ended—it remains as vital and alive as ever.

We need to shift our focus away from the hotel room where the shooter's body was found and instead examine the surroundings where the massacre occurred. It's striking that this tragedy unfolded directly in front of the Luxor Hotel, the third-largest pyramid in the world, named after the ancient Egyptian city of Luxor—a place famed for its temples, monuments, and proximity to the Valley of the Kings. Towering above this site are replicas of Egypt's iconic obelisks and a colossal Sphinx, structures deeply embedded with ancient symbolism.

Obelisks, historically symbols of power and spiritual guardianship to the ancient Egyptians, were believed to protect sacred spaces and honor deities, not to extend protection to Christian ideals. Here, these towering symbols seem to loom over the massacre as though fulfilling a purpose that runs counter to Christian values. In ancient times, these structures were designed to guard what they worship and to act as warnings to those who did not belong to that faith.

Under the Luxor's obelisks and Sphinx, both associated with watchful guardianship over ancient Egyptian beliefs, hundreds of concertgoers—many of Christian faith—lost their lives in a cruelly ironic contrast. It's as if the symbols were protecting the Luxor itself while issuing a silent warning to Christianity, standing watch over a tragedy that appears almost designed to align with a predetermined vision. The unsettling alignment of place, symbol, and event raises profound questions about intentionality and the eerie intersection of ancient echoes with modern-day devastation.

Pollack Hits the "Jackpot" with 777

The first shot fired by Pollack rang out at 10:05 PM Vegas time on October 1, 2017—just 20 days after the hidden 9/11 attack, a catastrophe marked by devastating hurricanes. But a shift to Eastern Standard Time reveals a different story. On the East Coast, specifically in Tampa, Florida, that single shot occurred at 1:05 AM on October 2, 2017, exactly 21 days and five minutes after the calculated assault of four hurricanes—Harvey, Irma, Maria (H.I.M.), and Jose—whose combined devastation led to an estimated $293.6 billion in damages and the loss of 3,216 lives.

The significance of "21" resonates deeply. A 21-gun salute honors the fallen, foreign dignitaries, and key figures, as a tradition rooted in symbolic luck. When you add 7+7+7, the sum is 21—a nod to "luck" in Vegas, where a 777 on the slot machine yields the "jackpot." In this case, Pollack's massacre acted as a twisted 21-gun salute, marking his "bloody jackpot" at the Route 91 Harvest Fest Massacre, with his "winnings" paid out in blood.

This horrific event seems calculated to echo the "9/11 hurricanes" and follows the five-year anniversary of the 9/11/2012 Benghazi attack. It's impossible to ignore the presence of the Egyptian obelisk in front of the Luxor Hotel, standing as if in silent witness. In parallel, the Washington Monument, the world's tallest Egyptian-style obelisk, stands 555 feet tall. The pattern continues with the hurricanes, each reaching Category 5: a chilling recurrence of "5-5-5."

If Pollack had started shooting only six minutes earlier, it would still have marked precisely 20 days since Hurricane Irma. Instead, he waited to ensure his attack began exactly 21 days later in Vegas, where the number 777 symbolizes hitting the jackpot—a fitting term for the orchestrators behind this massacre, who seemed intent on using a 21-gun salute as a tribute to the Hidden 9/11 Massacre by Weather Warfare.

Helter Skelter Comes to Nevada

In my other book, Camelot Murders and the Crucifixion of Mary Jo, I explore Charles Manson's Helter Skelter, which began on August 8, 1969 (8/8/69), exactly 21 days after the tragic death of Mary Jo Kopechne on July 18, 1969. Her death, a symbolic sacrifice outlined in my book, occurred in a Delmont 88—a car whose model number aligns with the start date of the Manson murders, 8/8.

Coincidentally, another eerie "mirror-image" murder occurred in Wilkes-Barre, PA, Mary Jo's hometown, 21 days before the moon launch, claiming the life of Joan Marie Dymond, a 14-year-old girl. These events and others are covered in depth in The Camelot Murders. For this discussion, however, recognize that Pollack's massacre serves as the third deadly 21-Gun Seig Heil salute I've uncovered, hinting at a common source within the Deep State—possibly involving the CIA and MK-Ultra.

In 1969, the Manson Family left a horrifying message at the scene of Sharon Tate's murder, scrawling the word "PIG" in blood on her front door. This brutal act symbolized Charles Manson's twisted vision, dehumanizing his victims as representatives of a society he sought to destroy. Decades later, echoes of this same dehumanization appeared in Las Vegas, where concertgoers at the Route 91 Harvest Festival were treated as mere "pigs" by an unseen force targeting them in cold blood. This mindset—a willingness to see innocent lives as expendable—persists in today's culture, often veiled in rhetoric that fosters hatred or treats people as obstacles to be removed.

Even public figures like Whoopi Goldberg, who recently referred to grocery store owners as "pigs," can evoke disturbing undertones, whether intentionally or not. The Italian-American LaBiancas, victims of the Manson murders, owned two cherished grocery stores, Gateway Markets, serving their community with dedication until their lives were senselessly taken. In a chilling display, the killers left blood graffiti in their home reading, "Death to Pigs." Such language serves as a stark reminder of the destructive power of dehumanization and the constant danger posed by an enemy within—a force that exploits divisions, breeding contempt and violence against those deemed "targets."

It's as if Helter Skelter migrated from Los Angeles to Las Vegas—from a "small" massacre in the American Century to a massive one in the Post-American Century. We must end this pattern and begin the investigations before it strikes again. The body count is skyrocketing.

What will it take to finally expose the full extent of the 9/11 Blood Trail, and can America find the courage to confront its own history?

May God Bless You and May God Bless America!
Robert J. Antonellis
Robert@Spirit-Rising.com
@SpiritRisingUSA

www.ingramcontent.com/pod-product-compliance
Lightning Source LLC
Chambersburg PA
CBHW070545030426
42337CB00016B/2353